108 Stitches

Also by Ron Darling

The Complete Game
(with Daniel Paisner)

Game 7, 1986
(with Daniel Paisner)

108 Stitches

*Loose Threads, Ripping Yarns,
and the Darndest Characters
from My Time in the Game*

Ron Darling

with
Daniel Paisner

ST. MARTIN'S PRESS ❧ NEW YORK

www.stmartins.com

Designed by Jonathan Bennett

The Library of Congress Cataloging-in-Publication Data is available upon request.

ISBN 978-1-250-18438-2 (hardcover)
ISBN 978-1-250-23264-9 (signed edition)
ISBN 978-1-250-18439-9 (ebook)

Our books may be purchased in bulk for promotional, educational, or business use. Please contact your local bookseller or the Macmillan Corporate and Premium Sales Department at 1-800-221-7945, extension 5442, or by email at MacmillanSpecialMarkets@macmillan.com.

First Edition: April 2019

10 9 8 7 6 5 4 3 2 1

*To everyone I've ever
played with or against . . .
I've learned from you all*

Contents

Acknowledgments

When I think back on my life in and around the game, I realize it's been a life lived in collaboration. Baseball is a team sport, after all, and we do what we do in concert with our teammates and coaches. The same holds true in broadcasting, where I work alongside all these tremendous professionals in the booth. And so it is in publishing. This book marks my third collaboration with my friend and co-writer, Dan Paisner, and it's been one of the great partnerships of my career, on the field and off. Together, we're especially grateful to Mel Berger of William Morris Endeavor and Michael Homler of St. Martin's Press, who seem to believe I have something to say that caring, thinking, *reading* baseball fans seem to want to hear. This time out, they've been joined in their extra efforts by a group of boundlessly talented individuals at St. Martin's, including Lauren Jablonski, Joseph Rinaldi, Joe Brosnan, Paul Hochman, Ken Silver, Jonathan Bush, Joy Gannon, Jonathan Bennett, Jennifer Enderlin, Andrew Martin, Sally Richardson, and George Witte—a heartfelt fist pump to you all.

For me, baseball is the most nourishing game outside of literature. They both are retellings of human experience.

—A. Bartlett Giamatti

You don't realize how easy this game is until you get up in that broadcasting booth.

—Mickey Mantle

108 Stitches

Warm-Up

The Ties That Bind

A funny thing, baseball. When you spend your entire life watching it, playing it, covering it, thinking about it . . . it becomes a part of you. It gets stuck to the bottom of your shoe like a flattened packet of Gulden's pressed to the concrete steps of a section of bleacher. And then it stays with you—you look up one day and you realize you've been trailing a fine film of mustard with every step.

A lifetime in the game—*my* lifetime in the game—leaves a certain trail. Better, a certain footprint. And in this way I have walked alongside every athlete who has ever put on a uniform, every coach or manager who ever sat in a big league dugout, every fan who ever played hooky from work or school and sat in the stands for a midweek day game.

We're all rounding the same bases.

This well-trodden path leaves me thinking, more than forty years after I left home for the wilds of New Haven, Connecticut, to pitch for a Yale baseball team that had once been captained by a left-handed first baseman named George H. W. Bush, who led the Elis to appearances in the first two College World Series, and had once been coached by the legendary Smoky Joe Wood, who had once been a teammate of the great Babe Ruth on the 1915 World Series Champion Boston Red Sox, who had once reportedly hit a ball over the center field Green Monster—440 feet in his time. Indeed, the thru-line that runs through our national pastime can sometimes seem to stretch a country mile—the combined length, not incidentally, of all those wool and cotton strands used to wrap the cushioned cork center of an official major league baseball, onto which those of us in the game might find the six degrees of separation that connects every player who's ever put on a big league uniform.

(Also not incidentally, that country mile is the distance sportswriters used to ascribe to the mighty home runs off the bat of the mighty Babe, to whom I am now inexorably connected, as I have shown.)

Upon further thought, it occurs to me that the intertwining of the collected stories of the game is a much richer, much more poetic metaphor than that flattened mustard packet, so I'll be going with this one, here on in.

Consider the baseball: that cushioned cork center, wrapped tightly with four-ply gray wool, topped by a three-ply tan wool, a three-ply gray wool, and then a thin poly-cotton thread, all of it held together by two cowhide covers, hand-stitched with 88 inches of waxed red thread. For a guy like me, who made his living on the mound, those 108 raised stitches that give the ball its seams were where the game lived and breathed . . . and *danced*. Let us not forget, it's these slight imperfections and variations in the stitching that catch the air and allow the ball to move this way and that, up and down, left and right. The slider, the two-seamer, the curve, the cutter, the sinker . . . without those imperfect stitches, hand-sewn in about five minutes by Rawlings workers using two specially designed needles, the ball would be a precise sphere, and all the ways a pitcher has been taught to spin and toss a baseball would fall away. The ball would behave differently, as it traveled from the mound to the plate—meaning, it would *behave*. (Or, *not*, which would in turn correlate to your time in the bigs.)

And so I've come to look on the baseball as a symbol for the game itself—because, alas, we've been knitted together by our time in the game, we fans and players alike, and as I was casting about for a conceit to stitch together a book of reminiscences I realized there was room on the baseball bookshelf for such as this. Oh, there have been some wonderful, yarn-spinning accounts from former ballplayers; behind-the-scenes looks at locker room and front office shenanigans from longtime baseball beat writers; historically based novels that help us to connect the dots from baseball past to baseball present. But I'd yet to come across a collection of variously connected anecdotes spun from the career of a baseball lifer—so I figured, Hey, may as well write one. Why? Because as the game changes I find myself reaching for ways to remind myself that it is also holding fast to its long-held traditions and time-honored characters, and because I've found over the years that when I'm swapping stories with friends, one tale often leads to another. The memories dip and swerve, like the arc of a cut fastball. They brush you back and set you on your heels and leave it so you're not quite sure what's coming. That's the feeling I want to bring across in this book. Pull on one thread, and another one starts to unravel . . . and another one after that.

Perhaps an illustration is in order. In 1982, at my first major league spring training camp, I spent a lot of time with **Dick Allen,** one of the most feared sluggers in the game for much of my growing up. He was the NL Rookie of the Year in 1964 for the Philadelphia Phillies, when he was known as Richie Allen, and for the longest time he was one of my father's favorite players, so I started rooting for him as well. He was the American League MVP for the Chicago White Sox, in his first year in the league, when he started asking sportswriters to refer to him as "Dick," which was what he'd been called by friends and family his entire life, saying that "Richie" was a little boy's name.

Ten years later, I was invited to Pompano Beach as a member of the Texas Rangers, and "Mr. Allen," as I called him, was a member of the coaching staff. He took a liking to me—although, frankly, I found him a little intimidating. (He scared the plain crap out of me, if you must know.) Mr. Allen asked me what I wanted to get out of my time in camp. I said I was hoping to earn the fifth spot in the rotation. He laughed. And laughed. Like it was the funniest thing he'd ever heard. He pointed to **Jon Matlack,** who'd been a member of the New York Mets' legendary pitching staff in the early 1970s, who had a guaranteed contract, and suggested the fifth spot in the rotation was already spoken for . . . by him. Didn't matter how I pitched. Didn't matter how Jon Matlack pitched. Mr. Allen said, "They're gonna ship your ass to Triple-A, brother. Just you wait and see."

It was the first time I was made to see baseball as a business instead of as a game, and I wasn't sure I liked it. At the same time, I appreciated Mr. Allen's honesty, which even on Day One in a big league uniform I could tell was a rare and precious thing. Baseball people can be misleading at times—outright liars, at others.

Now, that's just one story, but stay with me on this and you'll see how it stitched itself to another, when the business of baseball bit me again on the last day of camp that same spring. What happened here was that Rangers manager **Don Zimmer** called me to his office. He said, "Son, you've had an amazing camp. If we needed a fifth starter, you'd be coming to Texas. But we don't, so we're sending you to Oklahoma City, and in late April, you're gonna come back to Texas and be our starting pitcher."

He was kind about it, in a way that he certainly didn't have to be.

Understand, if you're a big league manager for any stretch of time, one of your talents has to be letting people down. It might not be a talent going in, but you have a lot of opportunities to work on it, and here Don Zimmer found a way to tell me I didn't make the club in classic good news/bad news fashion. He let me down easy—and, I must say, I took him at his word. I was as good as made.

I think I floated to the parking lot as I left camp. I jumped into the sweet T-top Datsun 280Z Turbo I'd bought with my signing bonus, threw my things in the car, and headed northeast from Pompano Beach to Plant City—the strawberry capital of the world, and home of the Texas Rangers' minor league camp. The map said it was a four-hour drive, but it felt to me like it took just a half hour, and yet by the time I pulled in to the Holiday Inn where the minor leaguers were staying; the Rangers had taken a big fat eraser to that late April start I'd been penciled-in to make. The light was flashing on the boxy motel phone by my crappy bed, indicating that I had a message. This was long before pagers and cell phones, so people couldn't always reach you on a moment's notice—it's a wonder we were able to communicate at all, right?

It turned out the message was from **Lou Gorman,** another baseball lifer—and another New England native, who'd been a prominent baseball executive during my days as a schoolboy ball-player in Millbury, Massachusetts, just outside Worcester. His message didn't say why he was calling, just that he was trying to reach me, so I assumed he'd heard I was coming to town and wanted to let me know that he was in town as well.

The players used to call Lou "Mr. Good," because of a peculiar habit he had of always saying things were "good, good, yeah, good." He was relentlessly positive, and here he answered the phone with typical good cheer. He said, "Yeah, yeah, good. It's good you called, Ron. I just want to welcome you to the Metropolitan family."

I had no idea what he was talking about. I should probably mention here that we also knew Lou as a bit of a wannabe wordsmith, could never quite figure out what he was saying, so it took a while for me to put two and two together on this and come up with four. The Metropolitans, I soon learned, was the full name of the team I knew as the Mets, who'd apparently traded for me in the time it took for me to drive from Pompano Beach to Plant City. Lou Gorman, I was also soon learning, had taken a job with the Mets as vice president of player personnel, working with general manager Frank Cashen. He was calling to welcome me to the club.

The first thing I could think to say was, "Who'd I get traded for?"

Even with just one spring training camp under my belt I knew the answer to this question was a clear way to measure your worth as a ballplayer. If you were traded for someone you'd never heard of, chances are no one would ever hear of you. If you were traded for a star, and if there were multiple players involved in the deal . . . well, then it meant that somebody, somewhere thought you might have some small thing to contribute to the acquiring club, at some point.

It was a little unusual, then as now, for a first-round draft choice to be traded away before logging a full season in the organization.

Texas had taken me with the #9 overall pick in the draft the previous June, and I guess they'd seen enough. That's how the game is played, I was realizing, and I was reminded of the uncertain, untethered ways I was made to feel as I took in this news when I read that **Dansby Swanson,** the #1 overall pick in the 2015 draft, had been traded to the Atlanta Braves less than six months after receiving a $6.5 million signing bonus from the Arizona Diamondbacks. I saw that and thought, *Welcome to the big leagues, kid.*

Lou told me I'd been traded along with another minor league pitcher named **Walt Terrell** for Lee Mazzilli, who'd been one of the Mets' most popular players during the team's fallow years in the late 1970s. It was all good, so good, yeah, yeah, very good, he said. For some reason, it gave me great comfort to know I wasn't being traded on my own. To this day, I've got no idea why this mattered to me—maybe because I wouldn't have to live up to the legacy of Lee Mazzilli, a matinee-idol-type Metropolitan, all by myself.

This second story connects to another—the story of Walt Terrell, who would clamber into Mets history after slugging two two-run homers off future Hall of Famer Ferguson Jenkins (the winningest Canadian-born pitcher in major league history!) in a 4–1 complete game victory over the Cubs at Wrigley Field. Terrell was famous among his teammates for the tower of empty Old Milwaukee cans that used to rise from the ashes of his evenings alone in his hotel room, which he spent drinking and smoking while the rest of us went out and got our nightclub on. We might have been on very nearly the same rung of the baseball ladder, but Walt was already a married man, with kids, so he would hang back in his room and wait for a few of us to return, unhitched, whereupon we would finish his beers and talk baseball. He was also famous for the time he tackled the San Francisco Giants mascot while the guy in the costume was running the bases at Candlestick Park, and became known forever more in our clubhouse as Crazy Crab, which for some strange reason was the name of the mascot.

There was yet another thread running through these stories, and that one was being pulled by **Mickey Rivers,** late of the New York Yankees championship teams of the late 1970s, who finished his career with these same Texas Rangers, but not before holding out on his contract and making himself a general pain in the ass, necessitating the trade for Mazzilli to potentially take his place in center field. During my one spring training with the Rangers, Mick the Quick was in the habit of parking his great big Cadillac just beyond the outfield fence at the complex. Just in case you weren't sure it was Mick's Caddy, you could tell by the steer horns he'd had mounted to the hood. Specifically, he was in the habit of leaning on the car horn, which he had retrofitted with a bleating air horn that made it sound like you'd stepped inside a circus.

Underneath the blare of the horn, my new teammates would swap Mickey Rivers stories like trading cards. He was, I was learning, one of the great characters of the game—and not always the most beloved figure in his own clubhouse, to put it kindly. When he was with the Yankees, he was known for hanging out at the racetrack. If he'd been to the track and had a rough day, he didn't seem to want to play when he got to the ballpark. If the Yankees needed him in the lineup, manager Billy Martin would get on the phone to George Steinbrenner and say, "Mickey's making noises about playing today, Boss. He took a beating at the track." Within minutes, Steinbrenner would send down an envelope with a bunch of cash, whereupon Mickey would crack the envelope, fan the wad, put it in his pocket, and head out to the field.

Years later, **Goose Gossage** would tell me a whole bunch of Mickey Rivers stories. Goose told me about the time he was being brought in to close out a game—back during the days when the Yankees used to drive their relief pitchers from the bullpen to the mound in a car provided by the team's automobile sponsor. This one time, as Gossage was being driven from the bullpen, Mickey crossed from center field and jumped on the hood of the car, screaming "No, no, no, don't let him in." Goose had been struggling at the time, and Mickey was always grousing that he had to chase down all those fly balls in the wide-open spaces of center field at Yankee Stadium whenever Gossage came into the game. Goose didn't appreciate Mickey's antics, to say the least—these guys really had it in for each other. Goose would scream right back at Mickey through the open window of the bullpen car: "Get your ass off the car!"

Once, the tension between these two came to a crazy head. Gossage came into the game in a tight spot. His thing was to start off every appearance with a fastball, so his catcher, Thurman Munson, wouldn't even bother to put down a sign. He'd just flash the glove when it was time to go—only this time, Goose was looking in, and Thurman was looking down at the plate, not putting up his glove. This went on for a beat or two until finally Goose called Thurman out to the mound. He said, "What the hell is going on? Let's go."

In response, Thurman pointed to center field and said, "Take a look at your center fielder."

There was Mickey Rivers in a three-point stance, putting it out there to all the world that Goose Gossage was about to give up a line drive or a long fly ball and that the great Mickey Rivers wanted to make sure he would get a good jump on it by setting himself like a sprinter. As it happened, Goose did give up a bullet to center, and Mick the Quick was able to dash under it to make the grab.

So there you have it—five or six or seven stories in all (depends how you count 'em), hung on this one line that stretches from Dick Allen and Don Zimmer, to Lou Gorman and Dansby Swanson and Walt Terrell, and on to Mickey Rivers and Goose Gossage, all of them tied up in such a way that I could never tell just one thread without telling all the rest.

This is how it goes, when it goes in just this way . . .

1

Drop and Drive

How far does this through-line stretch?

Well, for me, it reaches all the way back to 1883, when a journeyman catcher named **Dell Darling** had a cup of coffee with the Buffalo Bisons of the National League, alongside future Hall of Famers Dan Brouthers, Deacon White, Pud Galvin, and player-manager Jim O'Rourke. Darling collected three hits in 18 at-bats, over six games, although if you described his short tenure in this caffeinated way he wouldn't have had any idea what you were talking about.

A cup of coffee? What the hell was *that*?

This particular Darling would come back a couple years later and stick with Cap Anson's Chicago White Stockings, establishing himself as a reliable utility man, and he rates a mention here because of his name, which in a sidelong way also happens to be mine. See, like a lot of baseball-mad kids, I was in the habit of los-ing myself in the statistics and ephemera on the backs of the base-ball cards I used to flip and trade with my brothers. I was a sucker for baseball history, and with a name like Darling it was only a matter of time before I started scouring the pages of the *Baseball Encyclopedia* to see if there were any other Darlings who'd played the game. I suppose I would have done the same thing if my name had been Smith, or Jones, or Molina. These days, of course, I could do a search online and see if I shared not only a name but a birth-day with any of the all-time greats, or a hometown, or a hobby, but when I was a kid our search engines were pretty much confined to alphabetical order—a familiar crutch I'll lean on as these pages develop.

What's worth remarking on Dell Darling's otherwise unremark-able career, which spanned a total of 175 games over parts of six seasons, was how it ended—and, relatedly, how it bumped against a story that made an indelible mark on what was left of my child-hood.

Here's the front end of that tale:

About a year after his final big league game, Darling married a woman from his hometown of Erie, Pennsylvania, named Anna Crum. The couple wound up having seven children, but before all those kids started piling up my namesake made a whole new name for himself, when he was connected to a series of railroad heists that seemed to borrow a page from the stagecoach robberies that had once been a sad fact of life in the Wild, Wild West. Allegedly, Darling and the other suspects would hide out on these passenger trains, and while everyone slept or drank or stared at the passing scenery they'd toss luggage and other belongings from the moving cars. Then they'd hop off the train and double back to assess and collect their ill-gotten gains.

Quite a legacy, huh? No, it's not like we were related or anything, but I had enough trouble wearing a name like Darling when I was growing up, so it's not like this black mark would have done me any favors if I thought to mention this loose connection to any of my friends.

It turned out Darling's role in these robberies might have been overstated, because he was released shortly after his arrest, together with several of his former teammates, including a somewhat more accomplished ballplayer from Erie named **Lou Bierbauer**. With that bit of unpleasantness behind him and the stain on "our" good name not as bad as it first appeared, Darling tried to latch on with another professional club, eventually retiring to Erie, where he found work doing odd jobs, mostly as a blacksmith and painter. He died just after the birth of his seventh child, at the age of forty-two—quite possibly from the long-term effects of an old baseball injury, according to some newspaper accounts. What was curious about Darling's passing was that he died around the time his purported accomplice Bierbauer was widowed as well, throwing the former Mrs. Darling into the arms of the suspected train robber. Anna Darling wound up marrying Bierbauer, and the couple went on to have two children of their own, who joined the Darling kids and Bierbauer's three children from his previous marriage to form a bustling *Brady Bunch*–type household.

Some story. And the bridge to the *next* story I want to tell is that it marked one of the first times in baseball history that teammates ended up sharing the same spouse, a rarity that would serve as the backdrop to one of the most sensational stories of my own baseball-aware childhood. As reaches go, this one's a bit of a stretch, I'll admit. But when you follow the bouncing ball you never know where it might land . . .

In 1973, as many readers will surely recall, New York Yankee pitchers **Fritz Peterson** and **Mike Kekich** ended up trading wives, a domestic shuffling that confused the hell out of this twelve-year-old Massachusetts kid. Oh, man . . . this was a big, big deal, more *Peyton Place* than *SportsCenter,* about as far removed from a turn-of-the-century *Brady Bunch* scenario as you could get, and a sure sign to us Red Sox fans that the hated Yankees were in league with the devil. Actually, the two teammates didn't just trade wives—they swapped out their entire families, right down to the family dog. It was a weird, wild story, and a sign of the times, I guess, only at twelve years old I couldn't think what to make of it. It was exciting and lurid and a little bit creepy, and it had almost nothing to do with baseball other than the concomitant fact that the game just happened to be the place of business for these two friends and teammates. Still, whenever I heard the name of Fritz Peterson, who went on to pitch 11 seasons for the Yankees, Indians, and Rangers, or Mike Kekich, who pitched for the Dodgers, Yankees, Indians, Rangers, and Mariners over nine big league seasons, I was taken back to the Swingin' Seventies, where players wore shag hairdos and porn mustaches and wide-collared leisure suits that would have made their predecessors lift an eyebrow and wonder what the world was coming to.

Well, what it was coming to was . . . *this.*

For years afterward my mind would flash back to the tabloid headlines that had attached to this story, and when I was chosen in the first round of the Major League Baseball draft by the Texas Rangers, a team that had been Peterson's last stop in 1976, and one of Kekich's last stops in 1975, I thought about it yet again. Keep in mind, I didn't think about it a whole lot—it was just a fleeting thought, really, but once I learned what it was like to move about in the game, and to throw in with a group of twenty-four other guys in pursuit of a shared goal and our separate and hardly equal livelihoods, I began to look on this story in a whole new light. For some reason, I was dimly aware of this Texas connection, since I'd half-followed the career arcs of these two men with a kind of prurient interest, and in my own racing imagination at least it went from being a soap opera sideshow to an instructive lesson on what it meant to be part of a major league clubhouse. Surely, I thought, there would be players and coaches and front office personnel still active in the Rangers organization who had played with or coached or generally managed one or the other—and, I've got to be honest, I was wondering what it must have been like to hang around the locker room with these guys, when all of this was going down. Trouble was, I could never bring it up. When you're a rookie, you're expected to keep your head down and your mouth shut, so for me to have shown up in camp in 1981 asking all these Peeping Tom–ish questions about two players who had last pitched for the Rangers five and six years earlier would have been to call way more attention to myself than my plain station deserved.

Plus, it just wouldn't have been cool.

And yet every time I crossed paths with someone who might have played with one of these guys, I took note. Just to be clear, I *still* never said anything, or pressed for any details, basically because it *still* wouldn't have been cool, but a part of me was always dying to know what things were like in that Yankee clubhouse in that scandalous summer of 1973.

How do you look at your teammate after something like that goes down? What do you say to one of the "traded" wives, when she shows up at the team's spring training complex? Or, worse, when she brings her kids to one of those "family days" baseball teams are always hosting? Was it something you could razz a guy about, same way you'd throw it back at him if you caught him wearing women's underwear, or passing out after an epic bender, or was it off-limits?

Whatever it was that drew me to this Peterson-Kekich affair, I just couldn't shake it—hey, when you hear a story like this at twelve years old, you're stuck filtering it through the lens of an adolescent male child for the rest of your days. In fairness to me, I had no choice but to snicker.

One of the first times I encountered a former teammate of Peterson's and Kekich's was when I joined the Mets and was in the habit of taking my meals by myself at an Italian joint in my neighborhood—Pino's, run by a former Red Sox pitcher named Jerry Casale. A lot of ballplayers hung out at Jerry's place, I would soon learn, including **Mickey Mantle, Whitey Ford,** and **Billy Martin,** who just happened to be sitting at one of the tables one night having a big old time. I was maybe a couple years into my career, and this had become my routine, following a home game. I'd shower and dress at Shea Stadium, head back to the city, and stop in at Pino's for a nightcap and a bite to eat.

I've told this story before, most notably in my book *Game 7, 1986,* but I wasn't focused on the Peterson-Kekich connection in the previous telling. And it won't *really* make its way into this account, either, other than this bit of reaching and stretching in the setup. See, these three Yankee greats had all retired by the time of this notorious "wife-swap," but Mickey and Whitey had played with Peterson for a couple seasons before hanging up their cleats, and Billy ended up managing the Texas Rangers for part of Kekich's one and only season with the club, so these guys knew the deal. Plus, they'd been drinking—a lot—so it's not like they would have been in any position to judge me for trying to tease out this story.

But, regrettably, it never came up—and the reason it never came up (natch!) was because I was once again too chickenshit to bring it up. The thought ran right through my head, and left with the first round of drinks, after these Yankee greats invited me to their table. They knew who I was, I'd been in the papers, and they were baseball lifers at heart. One of them kicked a chair out for me and said, "Sit down, rook."

So I sat down—a baseball lifer in training.

We talked a little about the state of the game, about some of the Mets' young players, but mostly I just sat and listened as these old pals traded stories. Jerry Casale made sure the 7 and 7s kept coming. That's what they were all drinking. And drinking. I tried to keep up, in what ways I could, although there was no way I could match these guys drink for drink. I was drinking beers, as I recall, so I was able to hold my own for a good long while up against the three stiff drinkers.

For a moment in there, I told myself I belonged at this table with these Yankee legends, but this was just a foolish thought, and I was disabused of this notion almost immediately, as Mickey, Whitey, and Billy stood to leave, leaving me with the bill. The tab came to about $300—including thirty-six 7 and 7s for the old-timers. I'd lost track of our rounds by the time the bill came around, but it was an astonishing thing for me to consider, that these guys had each put away a dozen drinks and were somehow able to saunter from the bar without a shuffle or a wobble or a stammer.

In those days, I'd max out at about $400 in my checking account, so there was no way I could cover the bill *and* pay my rent, and as I walked sheepishly over to Jerry to let him know I was short, he smiled—said, "Don't worry about it, kid. Those guys never pay for their drinks."

It was one of those nights you want to bottle and set aside. Think of it: me, a babe in these woods, whooping it up with these icons, fitting myself into the rhythms and trappings of the game as if I had been there all along.

Probably the closest I ever came to asking someone about the Peterson-Kekich affair was when **Mel Stottlemyre** became the Mets pitching coach during my first full year with the club. Mel had been part of that Yankee pitching staff for a bunch of years in the late 1960s, early 1970s, so if anyone had a front-row seat to how that wife-swapping bombshell went down it would have been Mel.

What a lot of people forget about Mel was that before he became one of the great pitching coaches in the game, before he became better known as the father of Todd and Mel Jr., he was a stud. He made the All-Star team five times in his first six seasons, when a shoulder injury changed the course of what might have been a Hall of Fame career. He continued to pitch effectively for another five or six years, the ace of the staff on a series of mediocre Yankee teams, but I went and looked at the back of his baseball card after he joined the Mets coaching staff and I was blown away by his stat line—over 250 innings pitched for nine straight years! A staggering 152 complete games! The numbers were superhuman, compared to the pitching lines I'd see in my day.

My thing as a young player was to assume that all these former-players-turned-coaches, most of them All-Stars or Cy Young Award winners or MVPs, would be brimming with knowledge and hard-won wisdom. I was eager to soak up whatever they had to teach me . . . but that's not exactly how it worked. The algorithm of the game was such that you never really made any money, so a lot of former ballplayers would hang on in what ways they could to keep that paycheck coming. These days, the stars of the game are so well paid, there's no reason for them to stick around, so you wind up with a lot of journeyman types in these roles. I suppose this can be seen as a kind of blessing in disguise, because most of the guys who fight to hang on to their big league careers are paying good and close attention. They're taking notes, studying the nooks and crannies of the game in a way that might make them better prepared for a coaching role.

When I was coming up, early 1980s, most managers filled out their coaching staffs with their buddies, and the coach's job was to drink with the manager, in a sycophantic kind of way. After they'd had a few, they'd sit around and not-so-quietly criticize their players. My very first major league pitching coach, when I was called up to the Mets to make five starts at the end of the 1983 season, was **Bill Monbouquette.** Naturally, as a lifelong Red Sox fan, I remembered Monbo, a twenty-game winner who'd pitched a no-hitter against the White Sox, so I was excited to learn at his feet. But Monbo's coaching advice was essentially limited to two words: *drop* and *drive*. That was the style of pitching mastered by the Mets' ace Tom Seaver, who was back with the team for a second tour, and Monbo was the sort of coach who figured that if it worked for one of the greatest pitchers of all time it would work for all—letting me know that if I had come to these major leagues expecting to find a group of caring, insightful coaches prepared to coach *individual* players *individually* I was bound to be disappointed.

"Drop and drive, son," Monbo would always say—always, as in *always*. It was his answer to every situation.

I'd want to talk to him about how I might get this guy out, how I'd pitch around that guy, but this was all he'd ever say to me.

"Drop and drive, son."

Apparently, it covered just about every situation a young pitcher might find himself in, because I'd hear him saying the same thing to the other young pitchers on the club. (To the veterans, too!)

Mel Stottlemyre wasn't like that—no, sir. In fact, I'd go so far as to say that I've had three father figures in my life: my own father, Mel, and **Dave Duncan,** my pitching coach in Oakland. As far as baseball went, my dad didn't really leave a mark on me. Don't get me wrong, he had a profound influence on my childhood, and he knew the game, but he didn't know it well enough to teach me, so at fourteen or so I graduated from his tutelage and started playing American Legion ball, where the rosters were filled with college players and our coaches knew a thing or two. Later on, in time to coach my brothers, my father became a student of the game, but with me his advice had mostly to do with instilling confidence and discipline, and nourishing my love of the game and my taste for competition. He couldn't help me with my arm angle or my approach, so he had no choice but to kind of hand me off to my coaches—first in high school, and then again in a more meaningful way when I went off to Yale—and hope like crazy these guys would take care of me.

Some of them did, and some of them didn't. Mel did—in a big-time way. Best piece of advice I ever got from Mel was to think of a basket behind the mound when I pitched. A pitcher's job, he said, was to fill that basket with outs. That's all. "The good pitchers find a way to fill that basket with outs"—that was one of his go-to lines. Pretty basic stuff, but it takes hearing it from a guy who put up big, big numbers for the message to take.

Mel had a way with words—succinct, to the point, stripped of all bullshit or varnish. Another favorite saying of his was usually offered in answer to my frustration. He'd say, "Hey, the other team is trying, too."

Always thought that was a great line—and a great reminder that there was another team of rivals in the opposing dugout, and they were out to chase me from my game plan. For the rest of my career, I'd hear Mel's voice in my head, talking me through whatever sticky situation I'd pitched myself into, making sure I knew that those guys at the plate were out to do their best, same way I was out to do my best.

It was something to keep in mind.

Mel was what they used to call "country strong." We'd mess around from time to time during BP, and try to get the coaches to take their licks. We'd be at the ballpark early, maybe have some time to kill, so we'd coax these guys to stand in at the plate. There was always a lot of good-natured ribbing. We'd say, "Let's see what these old folks got." And Mel would usually win the impromptu home run contests we'd stage, against guys like Bill Robinson, but he was just a natural athlete. He could smack the crap out of the ball.

Too, he was the only pitching coach I ever played for who'd actually grab a mitt and *catch* the guys on his staff. He had this big old knuckleball glove he used to use, and whatever nasty shit we'd throw at him, he'd scoop it up like nothing at all. Whenever I had a couple bad starts in a row, and I'd be throwing to him for a while, I'd stop what I was doing and say, "You see anything, Mel?"

One of the tells I looked for as a young pitcher was whether or not I could see the *sink* in my sinker ball as it left my hand. To me, I'd always thought of that as a good thing, but Mel chased me from that notion early on. He'd say, "If you can see the sink, then they can see the sink."

What he looked for, he said, was the sting in his hand. He'd say, "If I catch you and my thumb starts hurting, your sinker's good. That's how it works."

'Nuff said, right?

My relationship with Dave Duncan goes back a little further than the first day I showed up in an Oakland A's uniform. Remember, Dunc was Tony La Russa's pitching coach for an incredible run of 27 straight seasons—a run that took the two from the Chicago White Sox to Oakland and, finally, to the St. Louis Cardinals. Before he became one of the game's most successful, longest-tenured pitching coaches, he was a big league catcher, mostly with the A's. That's the role he was in the first time we met, only I'm pretty sure the meeting didn't mean as much to Dunc as it did to me.

I was maybe ten or twelve years old, on a trip to Fenway Park with my Little League team. We didn't go to a whole lot of baseball games when I was a kid, but on this outing I remember trying to hunt down autographs—one of the sweet offshoot pastimes of our great game, yes? After the final out, I ran to the Red Sox parking lot with my friends, but we couldn't get near any players, so we made our way to the visiting team lot. We were all die-hard Red Sox fans, but we were equal-opportunity autograph seekers; we'd take whatever we could get. The Sox had played the Oakland A's that afternoon, and there wasn't a whole lot of security in the visitor's corner of the stadium, and I managed to sidle up to Dave Duncan, who'd taken over as the A's everyday catcher. He was out of uniform by this point, so I didn't know who he was, only that he was one of the A's players. He made a show of being gruff, or put-upon—but, really, he was a gentleman about signing.

I went home later and checked the legible part of Dunc's

signature—"D.D."—against my program, and I started following him in the box scores after that. It turned out, that was the only autograph I ever collected, so to wind up under his tutelage when I got to Oakland, it felt kind of *full-circle-ish*. (That's not really a word, is it?) And yet the thing about Dunc was that he wasn't the sort of guy you could tell that story. I could tell right away it would have embarrassed him. It would have put him in a spot where he would have had to show some emotion, made him uncomfortable.

Once again, it just wouldn't have been cool.

Of all the players I've been around, all the coaches who had a hand in my career, Dunc was the most clinical, the most analytical—this at a time when clinical analysis wasn't exactly the order of the day. He was the very first person I knew who paid attention to positioning and analytics, which of course has become a significant part of today's game. In the early 1990s, though, baseball was very much a game of instinct and tradition. Things were done a certain way—in large part, because they had *always* been done that same certain way. True, there were exceptions to the game's cardinal rules: when I was a kid, for example, watching the *Game of the Week* on television, I remember how opposing teams used to pitch to Willie McCovey and deploy what was known as the "McCovey Shift," but that was an outlier-type move. With Dunc, though, he'd look at the numbers, and let it be known how he wanted us to pitch to this or that hitter, how we should line up in this or that situation. He was subtle about it, didn't really call attention to what he was doing, didn't even tell Tony La Russa what he was doing, or why. Tony wasn't that kind of manager back then. He left it to Dunc to take care of the pitching, but if he'd have known his pitching coach was basing his moves on something other than his gut, I think his head would have exploded.

And yet for all his insight and instinct, for all his success as a pitching coach, even Dunc had to tip his cap from time to time and allow greatness into the equation. This takes me to one of my favorite Dave Duncan stories, although it's also one of my very favorite **Tom Seaver** stories, which is where the greatness comes in. Seaver was pitching for the White Sox. It was late in a game against the Baltimore Orioles. Tom was getting up there in years, close to forty, so La Russa and Duncan were looking on from the Chicago dugout worrying he was getting gassed. There were runners on first and second, two outs. Seaver fell behind the batter, 2–0, so La Russa flashed Duncan a look that said, What are we into here?

One of the toughest things for a young manager or pitching coach is to know how to handle a seasoned old pro with the pedigree of someone like Tom Seaver. The tendency is to leave him alone to do his thing, even as the "book" is telling you to make some other move, because while you're feeling your way into your role the last thing you want to do is show up a future Hall of Famer. These guys were all about the same age, had all been in the game about the same time, and yet they didn't have a whole lot of history together, so this was a tough road to navigate.

Sure enough, Seaver ended up walking the batter on four pitches, loading the bases and bringing up Ken Singleton, a veteran slugger who also was nearing the end of his long career.

La Russa nodded toward the mound, indicating to Duncan that he wanted him to head out there to take Seaver's pulse.

"You all right?" Duncan said when he got to Seaver's office.

Seaver looked at Dunc like he had no idea what he was talking about, why he was out there on the mound with him. "What do you mean?" he said—like he didn't have the time for this sort of thing. He had a game to pitch, and there was no room in his game plan for the kind of small talk Dunc seemed inclined to pursue.

"You just walked that guy to load the bases," Dunc said. It was merely something to say, even though he was stating the obvious.

Seaver waved him away—said, "No, no, we're good."

Back in the dugout, Duncan sat back down next to La Russa. He told the manager what Seaver had said. He added, "If he says we're good, we're good." Like he was reassuring La Russa while trying to reassure himself.

The two turned their eyes to the game. Singleton dug in. First pitch was neck-high. Ball one. La Russa said, "I thought you said we were good." Like it was now Duncan's fault, the White Sox now on their heels.

Second pitch was neck-high. Ball two.

La Russa flashed Duncan another look. He was not happy. They both started to think the game was slipping away from them.

Next pitch, 2–0, Seaver got Singleton to roll over on a changeup, grounding out to the second baseman to end the inning.

When Seaver got back to the dugout, La Russa walked over to him and said, "That's all for you today."

Seaver, professional that he was, simply shrugged and said, "Okay, Skip."

Dunc walked over to Seaver and said, "Boy, you had me worried out there."

Here again, Seaver looked at him like he had no idea what he was talking about—which, in fact, he didn't. "What do you mean?" he said.

"That walk," Dunc explained. "Those first two pitches to Single-ton."

Seaver waved away Duncan's concern—said, "I only walked the guy 'cause I didn't want to face him. I knew if I had Singleton 2–0, I could throw him the changeup and he'd roll it over."

Dunc told me years later that he was stymied by Seaver's response.

He might have seen it coming, but it just about floored him, that a pitcher could be so confident in his approach, that he would rather pitch with his back against the wall and no margin for error than to allow a situation to dictate the way he would attack a hitter. The lesson here, of course, is that great pitchers dictate the action, not the other way around. Dunc was so taken by the exchange he walked over to where La Russa was sitting in the dugout to tell him about it. La Russa didn't buy it, at first. He, too, had thought Seaver was tiring, and had somehow managed to dance his way out of a jam.

Later, away from the stadium, La Russa found a way to ask Seaver about it—knowing Tony, so that he could add to his growing arsenal of information on how to deal with a crafty old veteran.

By this point, Seaver had just about had it with these two guys second-guessing him. He said, "Boy, you and Dunc certainly don't have a lot of quality pitching around here, huh?"

To Seaver, this was Pitching 101. He was playing chess out there on the mound, while others were playing checkers—only, to exaggerate my point, he was Bobby Fischer or Boris Spassky, playing at the very highest levels, while the rest of us were fumbling along playing Chinese checkers. None of us knew what the hell we were doing, compared to Tom Seaver. And to this day, this exchange between one of the greatest pitchers of all time, in late career, and two of the greatest coaching minds of all time, in early career, stands as the best example of what it means to be in control of your surroundings.

It was a place I was lucky enough to find a time or two before the game was done with me.

2

"A" Is for "Aase"

When you've got a bunch of stories to share, the tendency is to group them in what ways you can—or, following the conceit of this book, to search for a common thread that might allow you to tie a bunch of them together.

And yet there are some stories that stand alone. They don't fit neatly alongside one set of stories any more than they might lead naturally into a whole other set, but I'm determined to share them just the same, so I'll lean on the alphabet for structure, every here and there—the lazy writer's approach to assembling a compendium of baseball anecdotes, but as you'll see it can be surprisingly effective, and I figure if I cop to it here my laziness will seem deliberate. (It's a little like issuing an intentional walk, yes?) To help with the *compending*, I've asked my friends at the Elias Sports

Bureau to identify all the teammates who played with me over my career—and in the pages ahead and in several chapters to follow, I'll invite readers to join me as I thumb through the resulting list of nearly three hundred names and see what book-worthy anecdotes come to mind.

What I've discovered, as you'll see, is that even though these memories find me in alphabetical order, they help to tap other memories and find ways to stitch themselves to other teammates, other moments, other remnants from the game's rich and storied past.

First on *my* list of former teammates, as he must be on hundreds of other such lists, is the alphabetically correct **Don Aase.** Trouble is, I can't think of a story to attach to Don, other than the fact that he'd been an All-Star closer for Baltimore during our storied 1986 season, and the fact that he'd made his major league debut for Boston in 1977, back when I was still in high school, cheering on my beloved Sox. Even then, story or no, I was struck by the Double A at the front of Don's name. I wouldn't say it cast him as my favorite pitcher, but it was a little unusual, made him someone to remember in this lexicographic way—same way a Red Sox fan of a certain age might follow Luis Tiant, say, for his unusual delivery . . . or Billy Conigliaro, for the way he reminded us of the career his brother Tony might have had.

It was a marker, of a kind.

Indeed, I have some specific memories of checking the box scores and following Don's career as I went on to pitch at Yale, and work my way through the Rangers' and Mets' minor league organizations, and each time it attached in some manner to the unusual spelling of his last name, my eyes pulled instantly to the very top of any roster he happened to be on.

By the time Don arrived at Shea Stadium, he was an 11-year

veteran. He'd signed with the Mets as a free agent ahead of the 1989 season, and we were only too happy to have him in the fold. He was incredibly gracious to the young pitchers on our team—to me, especially. He loved to talk about the game, about how to get hitters out, how to handle certain situations. If he didn't have a book on an opposing player, he at least had *an idea,* and I learned a lot from his approach. That was always a big thing with Don—to at least have a clue. And he was right about that, absolutely. Step to the mound and expect to blow the ball past hitters, and you're well and truly doomed. Develop a game plan, study your opponents' tendencies and weaknesses, and line them up against your strengths, and you give yourself a chance.

Don was only five or six years older than me, and I'd already had some sustained success of my own at this midpoint in my career, but our relationship was very much that of a mentor-mentee. And now, nearly thirty years after we played together, I'm still struck by the Double A of his name, which in the end wasn't even enough to place him first on an alphabetical list of all-time major leaguers. Wasn't even enough to place him second or third. He's behind Hank Aaron, obviously—and here he's in good company, because almost everyone else who played the game is behind Hammerin' Hank on some list or other. But he's also behind Hank's brother Tommie, which of course makes sense, and a journeyman pitcher named David Aardsma, who briefly toiled for the Mets during my time in the broadcast booth. That puts Don Aase in the cleanup spot on the all-time list, and he rates a mention here for the way his life and career—*his very name!*—stand as a compelling reminder of how difficult it is to leave a mark in the game.

Bill Almon was traded to the Mets early in the 1987 season, and one of the reporters covering the team pointed out to me back then that it might have been the first time two Ivy League ballplayers were big league teammates. Bill, who'd had an earlier stint with the Mets in 1980, went to Brown University, and he'd grown up in nearby Warwick, Rhode Island, so we also had New England in common.

A few things about Bill: One, he was the first overall pick in the amateur draft, coming out of Brown, which wasn't exactly known as a baseball powerhouse. Two, he was incredibly tall for a shortstop. That was the first thing we all noticed when he suited up with us. Three, he was one of the most relentlessly positive players I ever saw on the field. Or, I should say, *heard* on the field. He was an inveterate cheerleader. We used to call him "The King of Cliché," because he'd sit on the bench and shout out this endless stream of positive patter.

Show 'em where you live.

Get a good pitch to hit.

Take two and head to right.

After a guy hit a double, he'd holler out to the next guy up and say, "Trade places with him."

It was almost annoying, listening to Bill all game long, but it came from such a cheerful, positive place it became kind of endearing.

By the way, I never did follow up on that tossed-off aside from the reporter to see if there had been other Ivy League teammates— remember, I'm the lazy writer I introduced you to at the top of this chapter. I might have gone to Yale, and I might have been a pretty good student, but I was never the kind of pretty good student who went back to the library to fact-check the claims of my professors.

It *felt* like there was truth to the claim, and like a lot of American voters these days, that was good enough for me.

• • •

Tucker Ashford was a former first-round draft choice of the San Diego Padres (second overall!), who was trying to jump-start his career as a utility player when I was called up to the Mets at the butt end of the 1983 season. We were only teammates for a month or so—in fact, I think I played *against* him more than I played *with* him. He'd been in the Yankees organization when I was traded to the Mets, so our paths would cross whenever our Tidewater team would play the Columbus Clippers.

What struck with me about Tucker, and what has stayed with me all these years, was his name. *Tucker Ashford*. First time I heard it I thought it was just about the best baseball name ever. It's perfect, right?

Actually, the name works in just about any arena:

And the Oscar goes to . . .

With the first pick in the NBA draft, the Boston Celtics select . . .

Ladies and gentlemen, the next President of the United States . . .

So that's my Tucker Ashford story: I always wanted his name. Again with the names? Go ahead and blame the alphabet, for the way the Tucker Ashford entry appears almost immediately after the Don Aase entry. And go ahead and blame the game itself for the fact that Tucker's career never panned out the way you'd like to see for a tip-top draft choice. But his name? I'll take it.

Harold Baines was probably the quietest player I ever played with. He just did not speak. Ever. We became friendly enough as teammates that we learned to golf together on a municipal course near the stadium, where we sometimes played after day games.

If you look at Harold's numbers, you'll see that he was one of the greatest hitters to ever play the game—like, *ever*. But he never got a lot of love from Hall of Fame voters because he spent the second half of his career as a DH. If his knees had stayed right, and he continued on in the field, he would be enshrined with the all-time greats, no question.

Even on the golf course, Harold didn't speak. Our teammates gave him a wide berth at the ballpark. They honored who he was as a player and gave him the room he seemed to need to do his thing. But once we became golf buddies, I'd sidle up to him from time to time during a game and check in with him. One night, against the Texas Rangers, we were facing Nolan Ryan—and Ryan was blowing his usual smoke. In fact, it seemed like he was blowing a little harder than usual, felt to me like it was going to be one of those nights for him.

First time through the order, Harold grounded out, didn't look too good at the plate, and when he came back to the dugout I walked over to him and said, "Boy, he's really bringing it tonight."

Harold just kind of shrugged and said, "He's throwing all right." For some reason, he was unusually talkative that night, because he kept the conversation going—said, "I'm sitting on his change."

I heard that and thought, *Against Nolan Ryan?* You had to be some kind of hitter to sit on a changeup against a hard thrower like Nolan Ryan. (Long as I'm on it, calling Nolan Ryan a *hard thrower* is a little like calling Randy Johnson *tall*.) But that was Harold Baines for you—confident as hell, smart as hell, patient as hell.

Next time up, a runner on base, Ryan and the Rangers trying to hold on to a three-run lead and set the tone for the middle innings, Baines stroked a home run to bring us within one.

When he got back to the dugout, I went over to him and asked, "Was that a change?"

He smiled and said, "Knew I'd get one." He said he knew there'd a be a spot in the game where Ryan felt he needed to get him out, and that he would try to get him out with a changeup. "That's his third-best pitch," Baines explained. "And if I'm sitting on his third best pitch, I'm not gonna miss."

No, he was not—a classic example of a veteran hitter going up against a veteran pitcher, knowing that in a tough spot he would try to trick him, not beat him.

Billy Beane was one of my favorite teammates and running buddies. We didn't log a whole lot of time together in the bigs, but we were minor league teammates for a stretch. Billy and I expended an inordinate amount of energy trying to catch the attention of the prettiest girls we could find when we were out and about. It was like a challenge for him, to test his charms against the local talent. For some reason, Billy liked to do his sweet-talking in character—meaning, he would adopt some persona for the evening and pretend to be someone else. From time to time, he'd rope me into one of his charades, like the time we went out as two doctors from Cincinnati. Or, one night in Tampa, when he decided we would be two Canadian football players. He had our back stories all worked out in his head, and I'd have to remember my part.

I spoke a little French, so Billy decided I would be a defensive back on the Montreal Alouettes. He cast himself as a defensive back, too—from the Toronto Argonauts, I think. He even went so far as to cover where we went to college, and since most Canadian Football League players played college ball in the States, he decided he went to Alabama. He made me rehearse the whole thing, wanted to keep our stories straight.

Later that night, he was chatting up a lovely young lady in a bar, and he mentioned he'd played ball at Alabama and was now playing in the CFL. He threw in the part about being a defensive back—you know, for authenticity.

Well, Billy wasn't expecting any follow-up questions, but it turned out the girl he was charming happened to be the estranged wife of a former college football player, who was then playing for the Tampa Bay Buccaneers. This three-hundred-pound lineman had played ball at Alabama, so naturally the young lady asked Billy what years he went to school there. Billy was quick on his feet, so he threw out a year that kept him clear of the lineman's tenure, but he was terrified of being found out—terrified, too, of somehow winding up on the shit list of a bona fide NFL defensive end, so instead of sticking around to see where the conversation might take him, he high-tailed it out of there—me, a couple steps behind, trying not to laugh.

The moral of *that* story? I'll have to get back to you on that, but it's worth noting that the two of us were so young and arrogant and cocky we thought we could fool anyone—and, really, the only people we were fooling were ourselves.

M*ike Bordick* was a young shortstop on those great Oakland A's teams of the early 1990s. He went on to have an excellent career, enjoying his best seasons with the Baltimore Orioles, where he set a record for the most consecutive errorless games by a shortstop—110. I know this because I looked up his stats, not because it was one of those stop-the-game, check-out-the-highlights-on-*SportsCenter* moments we fans tend to burn into our collective memories—like, say, the way we all stopped what we were doing to watch Mike's teammate Cal Ripken Jr. break Lou Gehrig's famous "Iron Man" consecutive games streak.

(Remember, it was Mike who replaced Cal full-time at short, when Cal famously slid over to third base at the end of his long run as one of the premier shortstops in the history of the game.)

These days, Mike does color commentary for the Orioles telecasts on MASN, but I knew him as a young ballplayer—another fellow New Englander!—who wasn't exactly the best dresser. In those days, we all had to travel in a jacket and tie when we were on the road, and it was Mike's misfortune to have to ride the team plane with Dennis Eckersley, who was by far the best dresser in the bigs at the time. If everyone had suits off the rack that cost a couple hundred dollars, Dennis was wearing a tailored suit that might have run him over a thousand bucks. In today's dollars, he'd be wearing custom five-thousand-dollar suits, so poor Mike Bordick was looking a little threadbare next to Eck. And it wasn't just the quality of Eck's suits that put the rest of us to shame—it was the fit. Dennis had the perfect body for a 44-long, was movie-star handsome, and walked like all eyes were on him—which, typically, they were.

I imagine a lot of the young players were intimidated by the way Eck dressed, the way he carried himself. Bordy certainly was. He went out one day and got himself what he thought was a nice suit, just to keep pace. In fact, Mike was so pleased with how he looked in his new suit he stopped Dennis on the plane to get his opinion.

He said, "Hey Eck, what do you think of the suit I got today?"

Eck looked at Mike and said, "What do I think of that suit? That's one of the ugliest suits I've ever seen in my life." Then he went off on an epic rant: "Matter of fact, Bordy, who cares what fucking suit you have on? Do you know how hard it is to look like this every day? The suit's got to be perfect. I've got to have the perfect tie. The fit has to be just right. Who gives a shit about your piece-of-shit suit?"

Poor Bordy did one of these retreat-into-your-shell moves, looking away from the aisle, trying to make himself invisible.

Everyone in the couple rows next to Mike was laughing, hard, but what made it so funny was that Eck wasn't messing with Mike to be funny. No, he was messing with Mike because that was just Eck. He wasn't trying to belittle a young player or put him in place; he was just saying, "Who gives a shit what the rest of you wear? I'm a superstar. I have to look like a superstar every single day. Try that on for size, motherfuckers."

L*arry Bowa* signed with the Mets as a free agent late in the 1985 season, and it's fair to say that every single player on our roster, to a man, let out a groan when the news hit our clubhouse. I'd always hated Larry as an opposing player. I think everyone did—that's probably a badge of honor Larry loved. He was feisty, in-your-face, did whatever he could to try and beat you. Plus, he was an awkward-looking player, not at all smooth—but, boy, could he play. Over 2,000 hits, a couple Gold Gloves, a bunch of All-Star teams. But such a scrappy thorn in the sides of his opponents. I think I actually threw up in my mouth, a little, when I heard he signed with us—but then, as soon as he put on a Mets uniform, my opinion changed. Right away, I saw he was one of the smartest players I'd ever seen, knew the game inside out, upside down, all around.

And yet I include Larry here because he's the kind of player who might not get a chance in today's game. He didn't hit for power, wasn't a high-average guy, wasn't a classically gifted athlete . . . but the man could play. You could just tell he'd be a successful big league manager someday—he saw things *way* before they happened, and he thought about them *way* after.

He wasn't with us long enough to make any kind of impact on the field, never really had much of a role, and he hung it up after '85. But he made an impact just the same.

. . .

Ionly played a few hot minutes with **Dennis "Oil Can" Boyd,** the momentarily great Red Sox pitcher who featured significantly in the team's turnaround in the late 1980s. We were teammates on the Montreal Expos for a couple weeks in 1991—but we had a history before that, of course. Dennis was one of the workhorse stars of the Red Sox 1986 pitching staff. He'd won 16 games that year for Boston, and was slated to start Game 7 of the World Series against yours truly, before a rainout pushed the game back another day and left-hander Bruce Hurst, on closer-to-full-rest, was tabbed instead—here again, against yours truly.

In Game 3 of the 1986 World Series, though, Oil Can was on the receiving end of the ugliest piece of vitriol I've ever heard—in a bar, on a baseball diamond . . . *anywhere.* It was right up there with one of the worst, most shameful moments I ever experienced in the game, and one of the great shames of the exchange was that I sat there with my teammates and didn't do a damn thing about it. In fact, it resulted in a momentum shift that probably turned the Series around for us, and like most of the other guys on the bench I stood and cheered at the positive outcome.

Recall, the Mets had dropped the first two games at home in that Series—a nail-biter and a laugher. Going into Game 3 at Fenway Park, on the heels of that lopsided loss at Shea, we were feeling the pressure. I was tempted to write that we were *really* feeling the pressure, but this team wasn't like that. This team was arrogant, always believed it would win it all, never mind what it said on the scoreboard or in the box score. Still and all, it was a must-win for the good guys, only we didn't exactly come across as good guys on this.

The hero of Game 3 for us was also the asshole of the game—**Lenny Dykstra,** one of baseball's all-time thugs. You know how there always seems to be a guy in every organization, in every walk of life, who gets away with murder—*murder* being a figurative term in this case? That was Lenny. He was a criminal in every sense, although during his playing days his crimes were mostly of an interpersonal nature. He treated people like shit, walked around like his shit didn't stink, and was generally a shitty human being—and, just maybe, the most confident, cockiest player I would ever encounter. It was after he left the game, though, that his behavior took a truly criminal turn; he ended up being sentenced to house arrest on a bankruptcy fraud indictment, and he was also up on drug possession and grand theft auto charges, for which he received a three-year prison sentence.

Not exactly the poster boy for America's game, huh?

Lenny was leading off for us that night, as he did most nights when he was in the lineup, and as Oil Can was taking his final warm-ups on the mound, Lenny was in the on-deck circle shouting every imaginable and unimaginable insult and expletive in his direction—foul, racist, hateful, hurtful stuff. I don't want to be too specific here, because I don't want to commemorate this dark, low moment in Mets history in that way, but I will say that it was the worst collection of taunts and insults I'd ever heard—worse, I'm betting, than anything Jackie Robinson might have heard, his first couple times around the league. *Way* worse than the Hollywood version of opposing players' mistreatment of Jackie that was on display in *The Jackie Robinson Story*. *Way* worse than whatever Kevin Garnett had famously said to get under Carmelo Anthony's skin the night Melo went looking for KG in the locker room after a Celtics-Knicks game in 2013.

And yet whatever Lenny shouted at Oil Can out there on the mound that night might have had the desired effect, because Dennis looked rattled. It's amazing to me, looking back, that there's no footage from the game revealing Lenny's treachery. He was out there shouting this stream-of-unconscionable shit in plain sight, in earshot of anyone in one of the front rows, and certainly in range of the cameras and microphones that had been set up to record the game, but I guess the attention was elsewhere.

To be clear, bench-jockeying has a long and fine tradition in the game, and there's a fine art to it, but there are lines that are not meant to be crossed. Wives and girlfriends are usually off-limits, except if a taunt is offered in a benign, nonspecific way—as in, "Tell your wife to stop calling my room!" (In popular usage, offered by a beer-soaked fan taunting you from the stands.) Racial or religious or sexual slurs are typically out-of-bounds as well. For the most part, the razzing is limited to the target's physical appearance, or his skills as a ballplayer—as in, "You can't even run to first without getting gassed." Or, on an attempted bunt: "Who's gonna run for you?" Or, apropos of pretty much anything: "You ain't got shit today."

But this stuff coming out of Lenny's mouth was beyond the pale. Unprintable, unmentionable, unforgettable. And, like I said, he was landing his punches: first at-bat of the game, Lenny smoked a 1–1 pitch deep down the right field line for a home run, igniting a four-run rally, and setting us up to take back some of the momentum we'd lost in the opening games at Shea.

Lenny came back to the dugout and collected the high-fives and huzzahs that came his way, and for all I know I was right there with my teammates, thrilled to be back in this thing. It's only in retrospect that I started to feel somewhat complicit, and that by accepting the gifts that fell Lenny's way as a result of his ugly treatment of the opposing pitcher I was an accomplice, of a kind.

A curious side note: going into this game, the Mets had a history of momentum-shifting home runs to lead off Game 3s in

World Series. In 1969, the Series tied at 1–1, **Tommie Agee** got things started with a lead-off home run off the Orioles' Jim Palmer. In 1973, the Series tied at 1–1, **Wayne Garrett** took Catfish Hunter deep to start the game. I've often wondered, looking back, if Lenny Dykstra was somehow aware of this coincidental connection and didn't want to be the one to break the string, and so he looked to give himself whatever edge he could find before stepping to the plate and taking his licks.

Wouldn't put it past him.

My time in Oakland introduced me to some of the game's great characters. Cassanovas, too. High on both lists was **Jose Canseco,** who'd already been a perennial All-Star and an MVP by the time I joined the club. This was back before the taint of steroids tarnished Jose's reputation—and with it the reputation of his fellow "Bash Brother," Mark McGwire, who followed Jose's 1986 Rookie of the Year campaign with one of his own in 1987. The two sluggers were like princes of the Bay Area in those days— they could do no wrong in the eyes of the A's fans, who loved to watch them bash the shit out of the ball, and then bash the shit out of each other in celebration every time one of them bashed another one of their mammoth home runs.

What a lot of folks forget about Jose Canseco was that he had a twin brother named **Ozzie,** who briefly played for the A's as well. I'll never forget it, though—not *just* because Ozzie was still bouncing around the Oakland organization during my time with the club, but because of the particular ways he and his brother *bounced* . . . or, guess I should say, because of the particular ways they rolled.

My first wife, Toni, and I stepped into the elevator at the team hotel one evening, just as Jose and Ozzie were stepping off. We

greeted each other on the fly. They were in some kind of hurry—
off to paint the town Kelly green or gold, I guess.

As the elevator doors closed behind us, Toni looked at me and
asked if those two guys were twins.

I said, "Yeah, they're twins."

She said, "Well, they both tried to pick me up."

I said, "Welcome to the big leagues."

I've written a lot about **Gary Carter** in my previous books,
and the *missing-piece*–type impact he had on our team as we
took championship shape. I've tried to be honest about his reputation before he joined the Mets ahead of the 1985 season, the
ways we warmed to him in time and came to cherish him as a
friend and teammate. But there's no denying that "Kid" came to
the Mets with some baggage, most of it having to do with the ways
he was said to put himself front and center. In fact, there's a subject line in the index to my last book, *Game 7, 1986,* that reads *"Carter, Gary 'Kid'—spotlight craved by."* His teammates in Montreal
used to call him "Camera Carter," and that pretty much gets to the
heart of the baggage he carried to New York.

It's one thing to crave the spotlight when you're playing in the
frozen tundra of the Great White North, where the fans were still
kind of feeling their way around the game's traditions and nuances,
and where your teammates might dismiss you as a showboat or a
camera hog. (*Sacre bleu!* He supposedly went out and learned
French, just so he could give himself an edge in grabbing commer-
cials and endorsement deals! *Tres bien*, Kid!) But in a winning
environment, in a baseball-mad city like New York, those very
same personality traits can come across as positives. Being seen
as competitive, pushing your teammates to be better, playing with
flash and drive . . . these are good things, yes?

41

That said, it took us a while to warm to Kid, and here I want to share a story that could be taken as a knock but is offered in admiration, to illustrate the lengths he would go to come out on top. We were at Shea, a couple months into the season. I got to the ballpark early one day, because I was scheduled to pitch that night, and as I pulled into the players' parking lot just beyond the right field fence I noticed Gary's kids sitting on the back of his car. I was a little bit worried for their safety, because that lot was in the line of fire during batting practice. During games, too. Once, the Cardinals' Terry Pendleton hit a game-tying homer into the lot that short-hopped the door of my English-drive Mercedes, leaving a dent I would never get around to fixing for the way it reminded me of the heartbreak of a game that fairly knocked us from the 1987 pennant race.

I walked over to Gary's car, to check on his kids, make sure they were okay.

I said, "Your dad know you're out here?"

They nodded, barely looked up from what they were doing—and what they were doing, I now saw, was punching out All-Star ballots. This was in the prehistoric days of fan voting, when you would fist a couple punch cards from bins stationed all around the stadium and push out the chad that corresponded to the name of the player you wanted to honor at each position. Gary's kids had stacks and stacks of those ballots on the hood of his car.

Of course, I could see right away what was up, but I wanted to ask anyway—said, "What are you kids doing?"

"Dad's paying us for every All-Star ballot we punch out by his name," one of them said.

And that was Gary Carter for you. That was Gary Carter for *us*. Kid would do whatever it took to win. He wouldn't break the rules, but he would work them to his advantage—really, he was one of the smartest teammates I ever played with, one of the shrewdest catchers I ever pitched to. And here he was, gaming the system, unabashedly, putting his kids to work to ensure that he received his due. And it's not like he didn't *deserve* to be named to the National League All-Star team as the starting catcher. He'd been the best catcher in the game for a decade. But Kid wasn't the type to leave anything to chance.

He had his bases covered.

Most New York baseball fans remember **Rick Cerone** as a key member of those strong, headline-making Yankees teams of the early 1980s. He had a career year for them in 1980, finishing seventh in MVP voting, after joining the team in a trade that sent Chris Chambliss and Damaso Garcia to the Blue Jays.

"Puff" signed with the Mets just ahead of spring training in 1991, my final spring with the club. We called him "Puff" because of the perm he used to wear—which, in fairness to Rick, had once been the hairstyle of the day, even if it did look a little like the puffed-up 'dos the Brady boys started wearing in the final season of *The Brady Bunch*. (Forgive, please, that third *Brady Bunch* reference in these early goings—that'll be the last of 'em, I promise.) He signed as the backup to John Gibbons, who was slated to be our #1 catcher. Trouble was, Gibbons went down in one of our last spring training games, in a reckless collision at the plate that pissed off everyone in our dugout.

"Puff" was more pissed than most, and I sidled up to him as we boarded the plane for the trip to New York to start the season—you know, to take his measure, seeing as how he'd now be my primary battery-mate.

I said, "What's eating you, Puff? Why the long face?"

He said, "I didn't sign here to play 150 games. I signed to play 50 games. This is bullshit."

I thought that was one of the greatest lines of all time.

That flight from Florida to New York to start the season was always a little revealing. It was the first time this particular "band of brothers" would board a plane together and head into battle for the season ahead, and you can learn a lot about your teammates when you travel together. Like the time we traded for **David Cone** just before the start of the 1987 season. Coney joined the club in time to make one appearance for us before we broke camp, and it was the first chance we'd had to check him out. We didn't have extensive scouting reports like we do today, so we all figured since we'd traded Ed Hearn to the Royals to get him, he'd be the pitching equivalent of Ed Hearn.

Well, Coney pitched four innings against St. Louis in our last spring training game . . . *and he lit it up.* Oh. My. Goodness. His slider was nasty. His fastball was chumming, humming. I think he struck out seven or eight Cardinals over those four innings— he was unhittable.

We looked on and wondered how we'd managed to get this guy for Ed Hearn. It didn't add up.

When we went to the airport for the flight to New York, it was still the question on everyone's lips—"How'd we get this guy?"

It was answered soon enough.

As the plane was climbing on takeoff, nose up, Coney started walking to the front of the plane. We all assumed he was going up to the first-class cabin to talk to one of the coaches. In those days, on our chartered flights, the manager and coaching staff always sat up in first-class, reminding us in no uncertain terms that they were the straws that stirred our drinks, and that their drinks were served in proper glasses. Still, we couldn't imagine what Coney had to talk to the coaches about. He'd only just joined the team, he'd barely had time to talk to any of us, so we were all scratching our heads. Coney stopped at the first-class curtain, reached into the nearest seat-back pocket for one of those big plastic placard sheets the airlines used to circulate to show us where the exits were, slapped it on the floor of the aisle, and started surfing on it to the back of the plane.

I remember looking on and thinking, *Oh, that's how we got him.*

Kevin Elster, the Mets' smooth-handed shortstop, liked to think of himself as a ladies' man, and he was. He had those chiseled California golden boy good looks, and it used to gnaw at some of us the way women would flock to him when we were on the road. He was always talking about his exploits, his conquests, in a way that would probably come back to bite him in today's #MeToo environment.

Understand, I'm not looking to excuse or justify Elster's behavior here, or that of any of the other Don Juans I played with or against. I'm not about to explain anything away by saying it was a different time. We were, almost to a man, a bunch of arrogant shitheels when it came to women. No excuse, no justification . . . just *context*, and it was in this context that this Kevin Elster story unfolded.

Kevin had this thing where he would travel with an assortment of white cotton panties, which he liked to have his visitors wear when they came to his hotel room. He and I were great friends—after Eddie Lynch was traded early on in '86, he was probably my closest friend on the team—but even I started thinking Kevin was a bit much when he started going on and on about his escapades.

Hearing about his personal stash of white panties was just about the final straw. After a while, a group of us decided to take him down a couple notches one night in Philadelphia. We arranged for a cop in the local sheriff's office to arrest him, on the grounds that the girl he was with was underage—here again, not the most politically correct or gentlemanly behavior on *our* part, but in our sheepish defense we thought it would be funny as hell. And it was. The cop *really* got into his role, slapping the cuffs on Kevin and giving him the scare of his young, charmed, golden boy life—probably the worst ten minutes Kevin had spent on this earth, until we all started laughing and gave ourselves away.

First time I met **John Franco** he was in the opposing dugout for an NCAA playoff game. I was on the mound for Yale, pitching the game of my life—a game I would eventually lose 1–0 on a double steal in the top of the 12th inning—and he was in the bullpen for St. John's. We later became roommates in the Cape Cod League, playing for the Cotuit Kettleers. John was struggling with an arm injury, trying to correct his mechanics and pitch his way back into form.

We had a blast that summer, spent most of our free time at a local bar called Rascals that proudly featured "disco rock" as its musical bill of fare, and what I remember most about that time and place in our lives was that John was the only guy in the bar who was short enough to stand on the tables and dance without getting hit in the head by the ceiling fan.

What is there left to say about **Dwight Gooden**? I've addressed his career at length, on the air and in print, and every time I do I keep coming back to thoughts of what might have been. At his tantalizing pinnacle, during his remarkable rookie year of 1984 and his dazzling sophomore season of 1985, when he was all of nineteen and twenty years old, "Doc" was the best there ever was. Hands down. Case closed. Shut the door. Really, there was no one better. No disrespect to Clayton Kershaw, perhaps the most dominant pitcher in today's game, or to Sandy Koufax, the most dominant pitcher of my formative, coming-to-baseball-awareness years. Tom Seaver? Not even close—not if you're taking any two seasons off the back of Tom's baseball card and comparing it to these two seasons for Doc.

(And not if you're stopping to consider that Doc, at nineteen and twenty years old, was just a kid—a teenager dominating a league full of adults.)

Bob Gibson's landmark 1968 season was probably the closest we've ever seen in my baseball lifetime—the closest we're *likely* to see—but even Gibson's numbers fall short when you look at them through the collective lenses of context and history.

Here, take a look:

	GS	W-L	ERA	CG	SHO	IP	H	R	ER	BB	K	WHIP
Gibson	34	22-9	1.12	28	13	304.2	198	49	38	62	268	0.853
Gooden	35	24-4	1.53	16	8	276.2	198	52	47	69	268	0.965

Statistically, 1968 Gibson matched up pretty well with 1985 Gooden, but let us consider the variables. First of all, Gibson was thirty-three years old, in his 10th big league season; Gooden was twenty, in his second year. Also, and perhaps even more significantly, that 1968 season was famously known as "The Year of the Pitcher." Gibson wasn't the only one throwing blanks. Don Drysdale somehow managed to pitch six consecutive scoreless games, while the American League ERA title went to Luis Tiant, then of the Indians, with an equally minuscule 1.60. Run production was at an all-time low, in both leagues. Tigers ace Denny McClain won

31 games in the regular season, while his teammate Mickey Lolich managed to pitch *three complete games* in the World Series, against Gibson's Cardinals. (*Three complete games!*) And one of my favorite players, Carl Yastrzemski, won the American League batting title with just a .301 average, the lowest mark ever for a batting champ. The pitchers were at a tremendous advantage—not least because the commissioner's office determined that umpires would be asked to enforce the larger strike zone that had been established a couple years earlier and widely ignored. Following the season, Baseball's Rules Committee voted to lower the mound from 15 inches to 10 inches, and to abandon the larger strike zone experiment, and the balance between pitcher-batter performance was restored to historical averages by the 1969 season.

By almost every measure, Gooden's season was superior, eclipsing Gibson's when stacked against the league norms and accounting for the changes in the way the game was played, such as lower pitch counts and a greater emphasis on rest for starting pitchers, and the emergence of advance scouting reports and video technology to help batters learn a pitcher's tendencies. And yet for Doc, these two glorious seasons in the sun now stand as indicators of a career that lay in wait, a career that was effectively derailed before it ever really left the station. Gibson's outstanding season was one on a long string of many—his best, by a wide margin, but he was no less dominant in the half-dozen or so seasons leading up to it, relative to his peers, or in the half-dozen or so seasons that followed.

Perhaps the best example of Doc's brilliance during those two seasons came in a game in Los Angeles. It was early in the 1985 season, and we'd gotten off to a good start. We were atop the NL East, leading the Cubs by a game and telling ourselves that this was our time and that every game was important. The game was tied

1–1 going into the bottom of the eighth. We just couldn't get anything going against Fernando Valenzuela, but the feeling on our bench was that he was tiring and that if we could keep the score where it was we'd get to him in the top of the ninth.

That was *always* the feeling with this team. We were never out of it. Each game was ours to win.

Trouble was, the Dodgers had some confidence of their own—and a little bit of hometown luck. They somehow loaded the bases to start the eighth, without really getting to Doc. Back-to-back singles by Steve Sax and Ken Landreaux to start the inning, and then an intentional walk to Pedro Guerrero to load the bases. Any other pitcher, in any other season, playing under any other manager might have gotten the hook at this point, but Davey Johnson had faith in Gooden. Plus, there was nobody in our bullpen who could do a better job pitching his way out of this jam—nobody in all of baseball, really—so of course Doc stayed in the game.

Faith paid off: next batter was Dodgers first baseman Greg Brock, and Doc struck him out. Then he got Mike Scioscia to pop up feebly to Gary Carter in foul territory. Then he struck out Terry Whitfield to end the inning. All on just ten pitches.

It was the kind of showing that left all of us on the bench thinking, *You have got to be shitting me.* Really, it was an astonishing thing to see, and what was most astonishing was that we all expected Doc to dispatch these three Dodgers in just this way. It was a given. That didn't make it any less masterful, but if the inning fell another way I think it would have been even more surprising.

That's how it was, watching Dwight Gooden pitch during his first two seasons in the league. It doesn't happen too, too often, but every once in a while you catch yourself playing major league baseball and you see someone dominate the way Doc was dominating and you start to think, *Well, I'm a major league player, so what does that make* him? Or, the demoralizing inverse: *Well, that's a major league player, so what does that make* me?

For the most part, big league ballplayers are all playing at something close to the same level . . . that is, until you're gifted with a next-level talent that leaves you wondering what the hell you're doing out there. In the history of the game, the difference between Hall of Fame–type players and solid everyday players is consistency, constancy. We all have our Hall of Fame-ish moments. I had some great games over the course of my career. I pitched 13 shutouts, a couple near no-hitters. I had games where I struck out 12 batters, didn't walk anybody—you know, games that Hall of Famers have. Hitters have games where they go 4–4, hit a couple home runs. That's a Hall of Fame game. We can all dominate, from time to time. But the truly great players dominate *a lot*—more often than not. Over time. And in 1984 and 1985, Doc Gooden dominated . . . *a lot*.

I should know, because I was pitching behind him. This meant I got to chart most of his games. This was a privilege and a burden, both. It was a privilege because Doc was playing the game like it had never been played, pitching like nobody had ever pitched, and I got to absorb it in this up-close-and-personal way. I was *with* him, on each pitch. But I couldn't take what he was doing and attach it to what I would do the next day. I couldn't grow my game on the back of his, because I wasn't the same kind of pitcher. Our styles were different. Forget that our skill sets were different—we came at the game from different places, and all throughout those historic seasons I had to fight the impulse to try and match what Doc had done the night before. I couldn't blow the ball past these hitters, like Doc could blow the ball past these hitters, and if I caught myself trying . . . well, then I'd be headed down a dangerous road. I had to chart his game, and learn from it, and then wash it all away, because a lot of what Doc was able to do on the mound just didn't apply to me. It was apples and oranges. A successful outing for me meant something different from a successful outing for Doc. It's not that I didn't want to strike out a bunch of hitters, and leave these other guys on their heels, but there are a thousand different ways to get it done, and Doc's way wasn't necessarily my way.

There are a lot of people who can play the cello well enough to fill the seats in our finest orchestras, but there's only one Yo-Yo Ma.

Looking back, I believe the front-row seat I had at the front end of Doc's career probably hurt me as a pitcher in the short run. And it probably helped me in the long run. There was a part of me that wanted to keep up with the lead dog, you know, and at that stage in my career I thought *keeping up* meant striking people out. And I was able to push myself to that place, on any given night. I'd have these incredible strikeout games, where all of my stuff was working . . . but I wasn't really that kind of pitcher. I'd have to get people out in all kinds of ways, and it was only later on in my career that I was able to step to the mound and not even think about striking people out. There was also this unspoken pressure to keep the ball rolling—meaning, that whatever momentum push we'd gotten from the latest Doc outing, I took it on myself to keep that momentum going. You don't want to be the guy who kicks it.

In the end, Doc was the one who kicked it. I've been hard on Dwight Gooden and **Darryl Strawberry** in my career as an analyst. I've spoken critically about the opportunities they let slip away. I tend to paint them with the same brush, because they both shone so bright, so briefly against the New York skyline. They were each blessed with all-time talent. And they each squandered their many gifts before they had a chance to realize their full potential. Their nemesis? Addiction. It's something that needs to be addressed, and considered—not just in professional sports, but across all of society. We've gotten to the point where we all have people in our lives who struggle with some type of addiction, whether it's gambling or alcohol or drugs, and we need to keep shining a light on these folks, so that we might help them back to a place of purpose. To their great credit, Doc and Darryl have each done a tremendous job, in recovery, speaking openly about their addictions—specifically, about the *price* of their addictions. And that price, in the end, was legend. Their demons, their weaknesses, their struggles . . . they cost them a shot at all-time greatness. It was theirs for the taking. The two of them should have put up Griffey- and Ryan-type numbers. Darryl should have hit 600 home runs; Doc should have notched 300 wins, maybe 4,500 strikeouts.

They could have stood as role models for generations of young fans, but instead they stand as cautionary tales—reminders, time and again, of what might have been. We need only look at Doc's masterful escape artistry on that night in Los Angeles to see what these young men could do . . . if they'd only given themselves the chance.

3

Coming Up

I wish I'd had some sort of template to prepare me for the life of a big leaguer—a movie like, say, *Bull Durham*, which didn't come out until 1988, long past the time when it could have done me any good . . . or a book like, say, *Ball Four*, first published more than a decade before I signed my first professional contract, although I wasn't smart enough to read it until much, much later.

I'd never expected to make my living as a professional baseball player, and now that I was out to do just that it would have been nice to know what to expect.

What was notable to me as I embarked on my first full summer in organized ball, pitching for the Tidewater Tides, the Mets' Triple-A affiliate, was the collection of lives that had been assembled and placed in these same-seeming circumstances, in these same-seeming uniforms that gave off the false sense that we were all coming at the game from the same place, all of us headed in the same direction, with the same goal in mind. This was not the case, of course—and this one basic fact of baseball life took some getting used to. You see, every team I'd played on to this point in my career had been made up of like-minded souls. When Vince Lombardi uttered that immortal line about how winning isn't *everything*, it's the *only* thing—a line he probably pinched from UCLA football coach Red Sanders—he wasn't thinking in minor league baseball terms. Here at the Triple-A level, winning wasn't the endgame so much as the means to an end.

My teammates up until this point had always been about the same age as me, each of us on the upward arcs of our young careers, each of us hoping to help our team to a championship season. With the exception of the short season of Double-A ball I'd played the half-summer before for the Tulsa Drillers, in the Texas Rangers organization, my teammates had almost always come from similar backgrounds, from the same parts of the country, and most of us were hoping to get the same things out of our experience. Even at Yale, most of the guys on the team were two-sport athletes from hardworking New England families like my own, looking to parlay our Ivy League educations into advantages our parents could never have imagined for themselves.

However, there was no such thing as a shared agenda in our Tidewater clubhouse, I was quickly made to realize. There was more of an every-man-for-himself sort of vibe than there was the sense that we were all in this thing together. We played to win, yes, but we also played to showcase our abilities—each of us in our own ways. At times, it felt to me like we were at cross-purposes. One player's success typically meant another player's failure; for every promotion there was a demotion; for every increase in somebody's playing time, there was another somebody riding the bench. There were players five and ten years older than me, hoping against hope that their long-held dream of a major league career might still come to pass, and others who were still hanging on and hanging in there knowing full well that those hopes had passed them by. There were young men with families to support, and not-so-young men who'd given up on the idea of starting a family until they got baseball out of their system.

At bottom, we were all "good enough to dream," to borrow a phrase from the baseball journalist Roger Kahn—meaning, we weren't deluding ourselves *entirely* with the thought that we could hit or pitch at the major league level—it's just that our dreams were of varying shapes and sizes, and there was no way they could all come true.

And yet, to a man, we dreamed . . .

There was Walt Terrell, who as I've written had come over with me from the Texas Rangers in that Lee Mazzilli trade, putting us in the same boat for the next while—only, it was a short while as far as Walt was concerned, because he got the call to the big club ahead of me.

(He probably deserved it, too!)

There was **Rick Ownbey,** a surfer-dude-turned-pitcher-dude from California who would leave the Mets organization in the trade with St. Louis for Keith Hernandez that would fairly re-make our parent club, and who was known primarily for his ability to throw a Frisbee with his bare feet. Understand, Rick didn't just *throw* the Frisbee and somehow propel it forward in something resembling an intended direction. No, he would whip that thing in a tight Frisbee spiral—a toss every bit as accurate and purposeful as one an experienced Ultimate player might make with his throwing arm. And he didn't just *throw* the Frisbee with his bare foot. He'd catch it with his bare foot, too—an incredible bit of dexterity that could only leave me to scratch my head and think that if baseball legacies were handed out on the basis of poetic justice and uniquely awe-inspiring talent alone, there'd be a plaque with Rick Ownbey's name on it in Cooperstown.

(By the way, Rick also taught me how to play hacky sack—a typical West Coast pastime that looked only a little out of place on the feet of this particular East Coast kid.)

There was *Jeff Bittiger,* a short-ish, pudgy-ish kid from Secaucus, New Jersey, with a biting curveball, looking ahead to a twenty-three-year career in professional baseball that would include just four cameo appearances in a major league uniform. He was in his fourth year in the Mets organization when we were Tidewater teammates, so he had no idea of the vagabonding, backwater journey that lay in wait, and so he was as shot through with pluck as any of us Tides.

Jeff's career was a study in persistence, I have come to believe. He was a September call-up for the Phillies in 1986 and the Twins in 1987, and he'd go on to pitch in parts of the 1988 and 1989 seasons for the White Sox, but other than that he was a minor league lifer, pitching all the way into his forties. His last stint was with the Fargo-Moorhead Redhawks of the independent Northern League in 2002. There was just no quit in this guy. He never believed the writing on the wall was meant for him. What I remember best about Jeff was that he had a tremendous sense of how to get people out—but I guess he was never able to get enough of them out, at just the right time, in just the right way, to pitch his way into a sustaining big league career. Still, he managed to win nearly 200 games in his 23 seasons of organized ball (only four of them at the major league level), so in this way, at least, he'd make his mark.

For some reason, there was an unusually deep and gifted class of future managers and coaches on our Tidewater roster, including **Mike Cubbage** and **Wally Backman,** who would go on to build impressive résumés as minor league skippers, as well as **Ron Gardenhire, Clint Hurdle,** and **Bruce Bochy,** who would go on to post 4,092 major league managerial wins among them as of the start of the 2018 season, with four World Series championships and three Manager of the Year awards (one each!) to their shared credit—quite a lot of pedigree to be found in one dugout, at any level of the game.

Actually, I should probably amend the qualifier at the front end of the last paragraph, because that *some reason* was almost certainly the presence of **Davey Johnson** playing the part of our own manager—one of the game's great leaders, who in 1983 was just logging his time in the minors, waiting for an opportunity to do his thing on the main stage. Davey was always drawn to student-of-the-game types like Gardy, Wally, and Clint—and they, in turn, were drawn to him.

Bruce Bochy, whose hardly great claim to fame was that he'd once played community college ball with former *Saturday Night Live* castmember Darrell Hammond, was already gone from the organization by the time Davey took the helm at Tidewater, soon to embark on a brilliant managerial career of his own.

Mike Cubbage had pulled the plug on his playing career as well, but he went on to manage the Jackson Mets, the team's Double-A affiliate, during our championship season of 1986, and he would step in for Bud Harrelson as the big club's interim manager at the end of the 1991 season, a couple months after I'd been traded to the Expos, so our paths never again crossed on the long and winding roads of our intersecting careers. However, Mike earns a special place in my memory as the first person I ever played with who'd hit for the cycle in a big league game—he did it in 1978, as a member of the Minnesota Twins, in a game against the Toronto

Blue Jays—and I was struck by the ways that singular achievement had been stitched to the back of his baseball card, a reminder that each of us could be great on any given day.

Davey Johnson will surely go down as one of the game's all-time great managers—the winningest manager in Mets history and the first National League manager to pilot his team to 90 or more victories in each of his first five seasons. (His Mets career also comes with a neat little asterisk, because as a second baseman for the Baltimore Orioles, it was Davey who made the final out against the Miracle Mets in the 1969 World Series.) But as I've already indicated, in writing about Mel Stottlemyre and Dave Duncan as two of my most formative influences in the game—father figures, each in his own way—I tended to connect more to my pitching coaches than to my managers, and here in Tidewater that connection was to **Al Jackson,** one of my first mentors in the game.

Just to be clear, the Tides didn't have a pitching coach my first year in Triple-A. Jack Aker was the manager that season, and he'd been a former pitcher, so his idea was he could take on a dual role. The gaping flaw in this strategy was that Jack never took the time to actually speak to his players—at least, he never took the time to speak to me. This was a problem, if I hoped to grow my game and learn to pitch effectively at this level, and that's where Al Jackson came in . . . not right away, but soon enough.

Al's Mets pedigree ran to the team's inaugural 1962 season, when he went 8–20 for one of the worst teams in baseball history. He went 8–20 again in 1965 for the (mostly) same Mets team, this one very nearly as bad, and what struck me as remarkable about Al's early career was his dogged pursuit. I don't think he missed a start during the team's first four seasons, logging over 200 innings each year—a record of workmanlike resilience that would command a long-term, eight-figure contract in today's game.

It was Al Jackson who taught me what it meant to call yourself a professional ballplayer. He also taught me the splitter. I'll deal with the former first, because up until my second season in Tidewater I'd never really thought of baseball as a job. It was just a game I loved that I happened to be pretty good at. Yeah, it also happened that somebody seemed to want to pay me to keep playing it, but I didn't think about that when I was with the Rangers. I didn't think about it my first year in Tidewater. I simply accepted it as my due. But Al set me straight. Without ever saying as much, he got me to think of the opportunity I'd been handed and what it meant to rise to it.

He used to say, "If you treat the game like a job, it'll pay you back."

He also used to say, "Ain't nothin' gonna be handed to you."

In a lot of ways, I was closer to Al than I was to anyone else on those Tidewater teams. We weren't *friends*—ours was very much a mentor-mentee type of relationship. I don't think we ever went out for a beer after a game. But I enjoyed Al's company immensely. He was all business, all the time, but there was a soft, sweet side to his personality, and it bubbled to the surface from time to time. He had an incredible laugh that could light up the clubhouse, and he had a deep affection for the game that was fairly infectious.

More than anyone else at the beginning of my career, he was my pitching guru—Mr. Miyagi to my Daniel LaRusso, for readers of a certain age who might appreciate a gratuitous *Karate Kid* reference.

One of the biggest changes to my approach under Al's tutelage was how I handled my off days. I'd always been a hard worker on the mound, but between starts my thing was to rest my arm, maybe get a little light running in, and otherwise twiddle my thumbs until my turn came around again in the rotation. With Al, I started to realize that I was always on the clock. Each game was a chance to learn something new, and I got in the habit early on with the Tides of sitting with Al during games when I wasn't pitching. He'd break down the opposing pitcher's game, push me to consider his approach. He wouldn't do it when our guys were on the mound—I guess because as pitching coach he was meant to be championing their efforts, not criticizing them—but we'd scrutinize every pitch when the Tides were up at bat.

"See what he's doing there?" he'd say, leaving me no choice but to scramble for something intelligent to say, which in turn forced me to think long and hard for a piece of insight I could pass off as intelligence.

Second or third time through the order, Al would point out the ways the other team's pitcher might change things up. The guy would throw a curve, maybe the first one of the game, and Al's face would light up like he'd just seen a shooting star. He'd say, "Ah, he's mixing in his curveball now. He's got a good one. We're in for a heap of trouble, 'cause he's been able to save it till now."

And he'd be right—we'd be in for a heap of trouble.

Al used to compare baseball to golf. He was always speaking in metaphors, and this was one of his favorites. He had this idea that you can't really learn to play golf until you hit the ball flush. He'd say, "You can go out there and hit the ball, hit it thin, hit it fat, but you can't *really* play until you hit it flush." What he meant by that was that you'd just be hacking away until you learned to attack the golf course and place the ball where you want.

To him, pitching presented a similar challenge. He believed that you couldn't *really* pitch until you mastered the corner of the plate, low and away. That's the foundation of everything you're trying to do on the mound.

Without that mastery, he'd tell me, you'll never be a good major league pitcher.

With it, you give yourself a shot.

He'd say, "We can work on all that other stuff, Ronnie, but you know all the stats, 'bout what hitters like to hit. You tell me, if you're fishing and all the fish are on one side of the pond, where you gonna throw your worm?"

One of Al's great lessons was to get me to accept what the other team was giving me. First time he said it, I thought it was just something to say—you know, one of those old-school baseball homilies that don't really mean anything. But this was Al's way of telling me I didn't have to overwhelm hitters with my stuff if I could get them out with my second- or third-best pitches. It was a lesson that came roaring back to me one night early on in my major league career, facing Pittsburgh, when I found myself mowing through the lineup with just my fastball. Maybe it was because the Pirates hitters were so bad, or so eager to hit the showers on getaway day. Or maybe it was just that I was really bringing it. All night long, I kept thinking I'd reach the point in my game plan where I'd have to dip into that bag of tricks all pitchers carry, but I never needed to, and as I stood there on that mound, taking what these Pirates were giving me, I kept thinking of Al and those long, sweet afternoons in the International League when I learned to watch the game through his eyes.

Next thing I knew, I was shaking hands—thinking, This was the easiest fucking game I ever pitched in my life.

Al was a ball-buster when it came to fitness. To his mind, those easy games would only find us if we put in the hard work. He had us do a line-to-line drill, where we'd run from foul pole to foul pole. We'd start at a jog, then sprint, then dial it down for a stretch at three-quarters speed before walking it off. We'd do this twenty times, and to keep things interesting he'd lead us with these soft-toss throws that were just enough ahead of us that we'd have to really bust it to make the grab. It was a killer, that drill, but only if you went at it all out. A lot of guys, they would kind of lope their way across the outfield, and simply go through the motions of exerting themselves, and Al would never say anything to them. But after a couple weeks under Al's spell, I couldn't do that. The idea of letting him down was anathema to me. He expected me to give it my all, so I gave it my all, and when twenty reps did not seem nearly enough, I started doing thirty, and then forty, and on and on.

Al taught me to appreciate that being in shape and being mentally sound were the two parts of my game within my control. He also taught me the power of precision. The science of pitching, at bottom, is the ability to put the ball where you want it, when you want it, in the way you want it, so we would work endlessly on developing the muscle memory that can find you in the form of purposeful repetition. We used to end each session with me hitting my spots: ten out of ten on the outside corner, ten out of ten on the inside corner. If I missed, I'd have to start over, and what that teaches you, over time, is not to miss.

Learning how not to miss . . . that's the art.

Now, to the splitter. I'd pitched to only middling success during my first Triple-A season, left mostly to my own devices thanks to our noncommunicative manager–pitching coach, and as I watched several of my fellow pitchers get plucked from our ranks to join the Mets' lowly staff I began to realize I needed to step up my game. The 1983 Mets were a last-place, pitching-poor ball club, and I couldn't understand why there was no room on the big league roster for the likes of me—and, relatedly, why these other guys were getting the call, one by one, ahead of me. But instead of despairing or banging my head against the clubhouse wall, I had one of those career-changing epiphanies. I looked in the mirror and thought, Okay, hotshot. You're just not ready. And I wasn't. I was good, but not great. So I set about it, and in my newfound resolve to work harder I stumbled across this pitch. What happened was I was trying to develop a screwball, and even though I was making progress I was a long way from feeling confident enough in the pitch to use it in a game. The screwball came about because I'd been struggling with my changeup. Plain and simple: I couldn't get it to behave in the ways I wanted it to behave, so I thought I'd try something new. The reason I reached for the screwball was because that had been Al's go-to pitch during his major league career, which despite his won-loss record with the Mets was something to admire.

Al happened by as I was messing around with this new pitch, and we started tinkering with my grip and my arm angle, and soon I was throwing a split-fingered fastball. I hadn't meant to develop a splitter, and I hadn't realized one was taking shape . . . but there it was. Alongside of that, Al and Davey spent some time with me to undo the hitch in my delivery I'd developed in my short time in Tulsa. The Rangers had me pegged as a strikeout pitcher, leaning more and more on the hard slider and away from the three-quarters delivery I'd naturally developed in college, so Al and Davey set me up with one of our catchers, Mike Fitzgerald, and told me to throw like I'd always thrown, before the Rangers got their hands on me.

So I did . . . and it was a revelation. To Al . . . to Davey . . . to *me*. At the end of this one bullpen session, Al came over to me and clapped me on the back. It wasn't like him to get excited over the hard work that happened away from the game itself, but here he was clearly excited.

He said, "You got something now, Ronnie! You got something to work with now!"

Yes, I did—only, it wasn't enough to get me to the bigs just yet.

I didn't get the call to Shea Stadium until September 1—and once I did, there were a mess of new revelations in store.

I was "welcomed" to the big club by my first major league manager, **Frank Howard**—and by "welcomed" I mean to suggest that my arrival was hardly acknowledged. That was Frank's way, I would soon learn. He'd find the path of least resistance . . . and then look for another shortcut or two.

He was from another time.

Frank Howard was old-school all the way. He wasn't exactly the most cerebral manager, and he was disinclined to nurture or coddle his players. He wasn't particularly keen on baseball's nuances or subtleties, and I don't think he gave a shit about developing young talent or getting the most out of his veteran players.

I'll tell you what he *was:* he was tall—like, ridiculously tall. His baseball card had him at six-foot-seven, but he seemed to loom even larger than that. He was just a big, gruff, intimidating guy, and he terrified us rookies.

He'd been pretty intimidating as a player, too. He was Rookie of the Year in 1960, the year he came up with the Dodgers, and he'd go on to make a bunch of All-Star teams with the Washington Senators, and he was always one of those guys who made his presence known. His name stood out in the lineup card. He'd led the league in home runs and RBIs a couple times. He was feared as a hitter. You have to remember, this was a time in the game when players

64

were nowhere near as tall as Frank. Even NBA players in Frank's day were nowhere near as tall as Frank. Other teams had no idea how to pitch to him. And here on the 1983 New York Mets, no one quite knew how to play for him, what to make of him.

I'll write a bit later on in these pages about one time in particular that Frank's general cluelessness as a manager seemed to run counter to the best interests of the ball club and one of its most prized prospects, but for now let's just say that Frank was a peculiar guy. How peculiar? Well, he used to lift weights in the team sauna. In his jockstrap. It was actually hilarious, to see this giant of a man, damn near naked, pumping iron like that in the sauna, but we knew enough not to laugh our asses off. And this wasn't just a onetime thing with Frank. This was part of his regular routine.

Also peculiar was the way Frank would pack for road trips: he wouldn't. He traveled with a simple bowling bag, the kind Fred Flintstone used to carry, only Frank wouldn't pack a bowling ball. In fact, nobody could figure out what the hell he packed in there, because Frank never changed his clothes. We could be on the road for two weeks, and he always wore the same thing: white patent leather shoes, blue Sansabelt slacks, and a white golf shirt, tucked in. And it wasn't one of those stylish Arnold Palmer–type golf shirts that were popular at the time. No, Frank's shirt had a stiff collar that never seemed to lose its crease. He wore his pants high, like some clueless grandpa, but underneath his throwback outfit you could see he was still in terrific shape. You could see it in the locker room, when he walked around in his jockstrap, but you could see it away from the ballpark, too—he was maybe carrying an extra ten pounds from his playing days, but he was ripped.

The thing is, that's the only outfit he ever wore. Ever. He'd get to the clubhouse, strip naked, hand his clothes to the clubbie to be washed and hung out to dry, and slip into his uniform. Every day, he'd do the same thing, so in Frank Howard's worldview there was no need for a change of clothes.

Again, pretty hilarious—but, also again, something we knew not to laugh about or comment on or acknowledge in any way.

From time to time, Frank would step away from the ballpark while his one outfit was out of circulation, so he'd get dressed in his uniform and head out for a haircut, say. He'd sit himself down in the barber's chair like he was about to take the field, stirrup socks and everything, like it was the most natural thing in the world.

Once, he left the ballpark with a member of his coaching staff to make an appearance at a local youth clinic that had been set up by the Mets' front office. We were always being sent here and there on behalf of the ball club, reaching out into the community. Here again, Frank left the stadium in full uniform, which made for another hilarious picture when he found himself stuck at a tollbooth at one of the bridge crossings bracketing Shea Stadium. It was one of those old-style tollbooths where there'd be a basket hung out to collect your change, and Frank just sat there in the driver's seat, tapping the steering wheel, waiting impatiently for the gate to go up.

Finally, Frank turned to his coach and said, "Motherfuckers are taking a long-ass time to get me my change."

The coach, perplexed, looked at the manager and said, "What the hell you talking about?"

Frank said, "My change. What's taking them so long?"

"You paid the toll, right?" the coach asked, making sure.

"Damn straight," Frank said. "Five fucking dollars."

Yep . . . that was Frank Howard. A different animal, from a different time. The kind of animal who'd put a five-dollar bill in a coin slot and wait the whole damn day while wearing his whole damn

Mets uniform for the tollbooth gate to magically lift and his change to magically appear.

I heard that story and wanted to laugh my ass off—but here again, I was afraid to even crack a smile. We were all terrified of Frank—we rookies, especially. And we had good reason to be afraid, because there was one bus ride, early on in my first September sojourn with the team, when one of the veteran ballplayers at the back of the bus made a crack about Frank that seemed to make its way to the front on a wave of snickering. Frank must have had a sixth sense, to have been able to pick up on such as this. Or maybe he was just paranoid and had it in his head that any derisive laughter was somehow meant for him. Either way, he directed the bus driver to pull over, then stood up in the aisle, his big head practically kissing the arced ceiling of the bus, and lit into us.

He said, "You sonsabitches! You motherfucking sonsabitches! Talking about me behind my back like that! I'll tell you one thing, not a one of you chickenshits has the balls enough to come up here and talk that kind of shit to my face, 'cause you know I'll pinch your fucking head off!"

In all my time in baseball, then and since, I never heard a grown-ass man in what was ostensibly a leadership position scream with such cartoonish ferocity. His face was red, and I could have sworn there was steam coming out of his ears, and I thought, *Holy shit!* And underneath that one thought I could actually close my eyes and picture Frank Howard pinching the head from one of my wise-alecky teammates.

It was so . . . *right there.* And, like I said, it was so . . . *completely terrifying.*

The bus fell quiet, and the driver continued on his way, and I don't think I said a word to Frank the rest of the season.

I made my first start a couple days after joining the team—and as big league debuts go, this one was way more intimidating than the bluster that spewed from our clueless manager. I was due to face a Phillies lineup that featured three surefire Hall of Famers at the top of the order: Joe Morgan, **Pete Rose,** and Mike Schmidt. One, two, three.

As tough assignments go, this one had teeth! And hair!

I was staying in a crappy hotel by LaGuardia Airport on the night before the game, and as I tried to visualize and internalize and *actualize* the moment I wrote down all three names on a little scratch pad by the phone in my room. Then I tore off the piece of paper and brought it with me to the bed, where I looked at it long and hard. I lay down on the pillow, my head facing the ceiling, and tried to imagine how that first inning would go, against these three players headed to Cooperstown.

Morgan . . . Rose . . . Schmidt . . .

I spoke their names out loud. Over and over. I started chanting them. Over and over. I had no idea what the hell I was doing, or why, but I got it in my head that this was one way to stare down these all-time greats and psych myself up to where I could come at them the next day from a place of ownership, strength, confidence. Instead, I think I psyched myself out, and the prospect of getting through my first big league inning with anything resembling my dignity seemed less and less likely each time I ran through that list of names.

I wrote about that first game at length in *The Complete Game*—in fact, I devoted a full chapter to it!—so I'll thumbnail that opening inning here:

I struck out Joe Morgan, swinging.

I struck out Pete Rose, looking.

I got Mike Schmidt to ground out to third.

Then I walked off the mound to a standing ovation.

Indeed, there was a whole lot more to it than that, and looking back I'm sure the gloved hand of third baseman Hubie Brooks is still stinging from the screaming one-hopper he somehow managed to field off the bat of Mike Schmidt and throw down to first in such a way that the first ball put in play off of me could go down in the books as a routine grounder. Too, I'm sure the crowd's reaction had more to do with the promise of what lay ahead for the team and the young talent that was starting to fall into place than it did with any kind of command I might have shown on that mound.

I revisit the moment here for the way it bumps into an observation I want to share about Pete Rose, who of course never made it into the Hall of Fame after it was determined that he'd bet on baseball—and after former Yale president *A. Bartlett Giamatti*, now acting as commissioner of Major League Baseball, placed Rose on the game's ineligible list, effectively banning Rose from what had been all-but-certain enshrinement, and from participating in any and all baseball-related activities.

As a Yalie, I feel compelled to note that Bart passed away just eight days after issuing his ruling in the Rose case, suffering a massive coronary—and there are those who believe to this day that being forced to remove this apparent stain on the game he so dearly loved simply broke his heart. His death was one of the game's great sadnesses, and the fact that it was tied to one of the game's great shames made it sadder still.

It's easy for the baseball purists among us to dismiss Pete Rose's career on the back of his gambling addiction, but the Pete Rose I'll always remember from my playing days was a gracious student of the game. He couldn't have been nicer to me, whenever our paths crossed—couldn't have been more generous with his time or his insights. He had one of the game's most infectious personalities.

He played with joy and abandon. If you suited up against Pete during his heyday, you probably hated him, because he did everything at full throttle. He was out to beat you in whatever way he could . . . in *every* way he could. But if you played *with* him, or if you rooted for him as a fan, he was a presence to behold.

Really, I don't think I ever met a player on the field who loved the game of baseball more dearly than Pete Rose—a game he ultimately betrayed, a game that rejected him in turn.

Our time in the game overlapped at the twilight of Pete's career, so I only faced him as a competitor when he was already something of an icon, chasing history. If you remember, the last couple years of Pete's career, his story line was all about whether or not he'd break Ty Cobb's all-time hit mark. That had become his focus—and the eyes of the game were upon him as he pursued his goal. What this meant, as far as we opposing pitchers were concerned, was that National League umpires were loath to call a strike when Pete was at the plate. You could throw the ball right down the middle, and you'd never get the call. Nobody ever said as much, and it's not like there was this great conspiracy to help him along, but Pete clearly had the game on his side—not because umpires wanted to hand him the record, but because they didn't want to take the bat out of his hands while he was in pursuit.

Understand, it's not like Pete Rose was up there looking to walk. I suppose there'd been a time in his career when a walk *was* as good as a hit to Pete, but that time had passed. He wanted to get on base, and find a way to help his team win, but he wanted to get there by putting the bat on the ball. He wanted to do it on the merits. So if you had him 1–2, late in his career, you couldn't put the ball on the black and expect to get the call.

You had to give him something to hit . . . or blow it past him.

4

"H" Is for "Hodges"

N o, not *that* Hodges . . . the other one. **Ron Hodges**—
the Mets' (mostly) backup catcher, who'd been with the
team for 10 years when I was called to the big leagues
for the first time, on September 1, 1983. His tenure on the club went
all the way back to the Mets' "Ya Gotta Believe!" World Series team
of 1973, so he was a bridge from how things were when I was growing up to how they were when I was coming up. He'd played with
a lot of those Phase I Mets, like Buddy Harrelson, Jerry Grote,
Cleon Jones, and Tug McGraw—*and* founding Met Ed Kranepool—
so he'd been around, seen some things.

I was a student of the game, then as now, and I understood Ron
Hodges's place in Mets history, so it was a little bit thrilling to see
him walk into the dugout a couple beats after I'd arrived, dressed
as if for my first day of school, the white of my neatly pressed home

uniform looking like it had been dipped in fluoride. But Hodges didn't make an appearance in this story straightaway. He was more of a kicker to the tale—and it was a kick to the stomach, as you'll see.

A little setup is needed for this one, and it has mostly to do with getting the call to the bigs and reporting to the stadium for my first day of work as a big league ballplayer. Let me tell you, there's nothing like putting on a major league uniform for the very first time. It's one thing to wear the Mets togs in spring training, but to arrive at the stadium to find a jersey with your name on it, hanging in a locker with your name on it . . . well, it's one of the game's true *pinch me* moments.

(Go ahead . . . pinch me!)

I was assigned number 44, which would not have been my first choice, or even one of my Top 40 choices, but I was not about to quibble. That was a slugger's number (Willie McCovey, Hank Aaron, Reggie Jackson); a running back's number (Leroy Kelly, John Riggins); a logo's number (Jerry West). I thought it looked out of place on the back of a pitcher . . . but what the hell did I care, really? It was just a number, and it was stitched to the back of a uniform that fit like one of Dennis Eckersley's suits, and as I put it on I took the time to wonder how they'd managed to get my measurements exactly right.

These big leagues were a magical place.

It just so happened that I was the only September 1 call-up that season; the Tidewater Tides were still contending and the parent Mets didn't exactly have a pressing need for extra bodies, since the bodies they already had in place weren't going anywhere. A couple of my minor league teammates would join me in the days to come, but for the time being I was the only newbie in the clubhouse. At first, I was the only player *period* in the clubhouse, because I'd arrived to the ballpark early—like, an hour or so early. I didn't want to miss anything, didn't want team management to realize they'd made a horrible mistake and called up the wrong guy.

I dressed and soaked in the scene, the quiet and splendor of a big league clubhouse. If we had cell phones in those days I suspect I would have snapped a picture to capture the moment, but as it was I had to make do with my eyes and ears to take it all in and file it away for posterity—and now, going on thirty-five years later, the watery eye of memory tells me I moved about that room like I belonged. In truth, that's not how it was. I was tentative as hell, careful not to touch or upset anything or anyone. I knew a few players from spring training, but only enough to nod hello, so as these *actual* Mets started to trickle in and get ready for the game I flashed a couple tentative-but-knowing smiles, maybe said "Hey" a time or two, tried to play it cool.

When you're a rookie, you're careful not to step out of line, not to call too much attention to yourself, so I was definitely hanging back, and if someone was kind enough to offer a handshake in greeting, I was only too happy to take it. That's kind of where I was in my thinking when I wandered from the clubhouse to the dugout. I wasn't scheduled to make my first start for a few days, but I wanted to check out the field, see what Shea Stadium looked like—what it *felt* like!—from the players' seats. I was the only one there, didn't really have a job to do that day except to familiarize myself with these new surroundings and try not to come off as an overanxious fool, so I sat down on the bench and imagined myself into the scene. It's telling, looking back, that even though I was actually *in* the scene, I was still thinking a dream was required.

One by one, the Mets players spilled in from the clubhouse, and the dugout started to fill with the hum of pregame chatter. Nobody really paid any attention to me. I was just sitting off to the side, taking it all in, and it was then that I noticed Ron Hodges—the *lesser* Hodges, as what happened next would reveal. He'd been out in the bullpen, warming up the pitcher, and he'd just walked across the field to get himself situated. What I was realizing, in these early moments, was that major league ballplayers were creatures of habit, believers in routine. Everyone seemed to have a spot on the bench they liked, a series of warm-ups they fell into without thinking, a way they liked to park their gear. Ron Hodges was just going through his usual motions, such as they were, and at some point he took note of this Day One rookie, sitting ramrod straight in his starch-white uniform with the slugger's number on the back, looking brand spanking new and (probably) completely out of place.

He started to walk over to me—and, greenie that I was, my first thought was that he was coming over to say hello.

Yeah, right.

Oh, I was in his sights. And he *was* coming over to greet me . . . I guess. It's the way he did it that I found surprising, and more than a little dispiriting. He stopped about a foot away from where I was sitting, still just a handshake's reach away. But Ron Hodges didn't extend his hand. He didn't say a word, didn't even make eye contact. Instead, he suck-whistled on the considerable store of tobacco juice he had working in his cheeks, turned ever-so-slightly to face me, and sent a stream of the stuff hurtling toward my virgin uniform. A thick, brown wad of tobacco spittle alighted on my pant leg, where it immediately formed a kind of Rorschach ink blot pattern that looked, from a distance, like my thigh had the runs.

I was stunned, mortified. I couldn't think how to respond, except to look around and see if anyone else was looking, if I was maybe on the receiving end of some joke—you know, one of those rookie hazing moments I'd been told to expect. But this was no joke. There was no one paying attention—even Hodges had moved on to go about his business, now that he could scratch *spit on the new guy* from his to-do list.

The asshole didn't say a word, didn't crack a smile, didn't give away any tic or look or gesture to suggest that he was simply razzing me and that such as this was all in good fun. No, he just shot this wad of tobacco juice and turned away—a *spit-and-run* that left me feeling like a humiliated piece of shit.

So I just sat there, embarrassed as hell, terrified to move from my shame for fear of making things worse. I'd only been issued the one uniform, so it's not like I could have retreated to the clubhouse for a new pair of pants, and I worried that if I moved to rub or blot out the stain I'd be marked as a different kind of coward. So I just sat there, like an idiot, awash in the ignominy of the moment, and for the duration of that first game I tried to casually cover the stain by resting my elbow or forearm on my thigh, by crossing my leg over the "wound" or draping my jacket across my lap, the whole time thinking, What the fuck am I into here?

I opened the 1992 season with back-to-back starts against the Kansas City Royals. The first game, at Oakland, went pretty well. I took a shutout into the ninth with a 5–0 lead, and Dennis Eckersley was able to seal the deal for us after I gave up a walk to George Brett and a two-run homer to Jim Eisenreich to start the inning.

So far, so good.

The second game, at Kansas City, did not go so well. Oh, I got off to another strong start, even had a no-hitter going into the eighth, but then the wheels kind of fell off, which takes me to my favorite **Rick Honeycutt** story. It's also one of my best "game that got away" stories, although "best" is probably not the right adjective, so perhaps I should call it the most illustrative.

Now, in fairness to Rick, who went on to become one of the most respected pitching coaches in the game, he was a much better pitcher (and fielder!) than this hard-luck story suggests—hey, you don't rack up a twenty-one-year career as a big league pitcher unless you know how to get people out, right? However, the hard luck in this case was mostly mine. I allowed a lead-off single in the eighth to Keith Miller, my old Mets teammate, and with the no-hitter off the table Tony La Russa decided I was done. I'd thrown over a hundred pitches, we were at the front end of a long season, and he wanted to push whatever buttons managers push when they're trying to preserve a one-run lead. Also, I suspect he thought a left-hander would do a better job keeping a speedster like Miller close at first base, even though holding runners had long been one of my strengths as a pitcher.

I always hated to leave a tight game, especially after I'd pitched well and was still throwing hard, but I can understand La Russa's thinking—at least, all these years later, I can understand it. At the time, I was probably pissed, but he handed the ball to Rick Honeycutt to finish the inning, most likely thinking that if everything went according to plan he would then hand the ball over to Eck in the ninth to close things out. Only that's not exactly how things worked out. The next batter was Chris Gwynn, Tony's brother, who squared to bunt. That was the correct baseball move in this spot, to push the runner into scoring position. The other correct move was to throw over to first, to see if you could get the batter to tip his hand. Trouble was, Rick fielded the ball and made an errant throw, putting runners on first and second with nobody out. Terry Shumpert followed in a similar spot, and he too squared to bunt—

resulting in a botched fielder's choice that left all three runners on base, with nobody out.

This was where things got interesting—or, I should say, maddening. Honeycutt threw a wild pitch to Brian McCrae, and Miller dashed down the line to score, with Gwynn crossing over to third. My 1–0 lead was shot. Then he threw another wild pitch, and Gwynn sprinted home, costing us the game.

Just like that, in a span of a handful of pitches, a batted ball never leaving the infield, my strong start was erased—one of the emptiest feelings you can have as a starting pitcher. It feels a little bit like you weren't there at all. That said, you always want to give a relief pitcher some room when he coughs up one of your leads late in the game. Inside, you're seething, reeling, but the correct baseball move is to play it cool, pat the guy on the back, tell him you'll get him next time. And that's what I did here—went up to Rick as he came off the mound at the end of the inning and tried to pick him up.

I waited a couple days before I started busting his balls—and now, as I write this, it's been twenty-five years and I'm still busting his balls over this one. Just sayin'.

This strong outing in Kansas City wasn't the only time I took a no-hitter into the eighth inning. No, I could never quite get it together to pitch my way into baseball history with a complete game no-hitter, but I did manage to throw 11 innings of no-hit ball in college, and to go deep in a bunch of other big league games without letting up a hit. Curiously, improbably, I threw *two* two-hit shutouts in the span of two weeks in 1992, against the same team, and in both games the no-no was broken up late by the same batter. (What are the odds?) **Candy Maldonado** of the Toronto Blue Jays, who would go on to beat us A's in the ALCS later that season on their way to a World Series title, did the dishonor each time out—once in the eighth inning, and once in the seventh. The games were wrapped around a 1–0 complete game loss to the New York Yankees—all in all, a fine and formidable stretch that nevertheless continues to rankle for the way they stand in my rearview mirror as stark reminders of what might have been.

Like the game that got away that night in Kansas City . . .

Dann Howitt was a teammate of mine in Oakland, a career .194 hitter who would go on to earn a glorious spot in the annals of baseball history. Perhaps I overstate: it was more of an inglorious footnote, offering an unlikely capper to a Hall of Fame career, but it was memorable just the same.

Dann bounced around the bigs over parts of six seasons. I knew him as a kid from Battle Creek, Michigan—which, like most everyone from my generation, I associated with my favorite Kellogg's cereal. He was a tall, skinny kid, who could never really crack Tony La Russa's lineup, but he was one of the smartest guys on that Oakland team. After leaving Oakland, he played for a stretch in Seattle, and for the Chicago White Sox. It was while playing for the Mariners, toward the end of the 1993 season, that he stepped into posterity. Last week of the season, he was in the lineup against Nolan Ryan, who was due to retire at the end of the campaign.

Ryan was still throwing gas, but on this night he struggled to get out of the first inning. He gave up a single to Mariners shortstop, Omar Vizquel, to lead off the game. Vizquel promptly stole second. Ryan then walked the next two hitters, Rich Amaral and Ken Griffey Jr., to load the bases. And then, for good measure, he walked Jay Buhner to push home Vizquel with the first run of the game.

That brought Dann Howitt to the plate with the bases loaded, nobody out. And what did this smart, skinny, light-hitting left-fielder from Battle Creek do in that spot? He sent a 2–2 pitch deep to left for the first (and only!) grand slam of his career . . . off one of the greatest pitchers to ever take the mound.

What made that moment *momentous* was that Ryan was pulled from the game while pitching to the next batter—my old Mets teammate Dave Magadan. And, it turned out, that was the last game Nolan Ryan ever pitched, so with that one mighty swing Dann Howitt made himself the answer to a couple of all-time trivia questions.

Pretty cool.

Long as I'm on it, let me just slip in a footnote to this footnote. I wrote earlier that Dann was one of the smartest players on those A's teams of the early 1990s. But there were a lot of unusually smart players in that clubhouse—perhaps because Tony La Russa himself was pretty damn smart and was drawn to well-rounded players who could think for themselves and were able to develop interests away from the field. One of the other smart players was our shortstop, **Walt Weiss,** who would of course go on to become a big league manager—an accomplishment that doesn't necessarily anoint you with smarts, as we have seen with a few stories I've already shared, but it can be a leading indicator.

In Walt's case, though, the two certainly went hand in hand, and I can remember being made aware of the depth of his knowledge and the size of his memory during an afternoon game when the two of us were seated next to each other in the A's dugout. Walt was out with an injury at the time, and since I wasn't pitching or charting there wasn't much for me to do on the bench, so I was only too happy to sit with him and shoot the shit. I used to love hanging with Walt—he'd grown up in upstate New York, about an hour north of the city, and we were wired in a lot of the same ways. At some point, our talk turned to Bob Dylan—as it was wont to do in the dog days of summer when there's not a whole lot on the line other than where you might get dinner after the game. Walt let on that *Blood on the Tracks* was his favorite album, and I agreed that it was one of Dylan's best. We also agreed that "Tangled Up in Blue" was, like, one of the greatest Dylan songs ever, ever, ever.

Walt said he knew all the words—and to prove it, he started singing. He wasn't bragging, or showing off, but he was certainly singing. Right there in the middle of the game—not at the top of his lungs, mind you, but loud enough. Our guys were in the field (I think), so the dugout was not as full as it might have been, but it must have been an incongruous thing for anyone else on the bench to turn their attention our way and hear Walt Weiss doing a quite reasonable Bob Dylan cover—a cappella, of course.

I tried to match him line for line, but I fell off somewhere in the first verse, right around that part where Papa's bankbook wasn't big enough. Walt kept going, though. All the way through to the end:

> *All the people we used to know*
> *They're an illusion to me now . . .*

It was the most remarkable thing—one of my most cherished in-game memories. And it's a memory that lingers and sweetens with time, because whenever that song plays on the radio I'm taken back to the A's dugout, and somewhere beneath Dylan's dense, meandering lyric there's an image of these two young athletes, playing a game they loved, having the time of their lives, and swapping songs like they were back in high school.

Gregg Jefferies was an amazing young talent, one of the best switch-hitters I ever saw. Trouble was, he was a kid without a position, and without a sense of humor. He came up to the wrong team at the wrong time. There just wasn't a good fit for him on those Mets rosters of the late 1980s—playing-wise and personality-wise. Remember how I wrote earlier about how tentative I felt as a rookie? About me not wanting to stand out, or call attention to myself in any way? Well, Gregg wasn't like that. He'd been a highly touted prospect—the first two-time winner of *Baseball America*'s Minor League Player of the Year award—and when he joined the club to stick late in our division-winning 1988 season, he seemed to take himself a little too seriously.

He didn't *do* tentative, apparently.

Naturally, some of our guys gave Gregg a hard time. They rode him about the self-important way he carried himself, about how he never smiled. They even rode him about that extra "g" at the end of his first name—because, you know, ballplayers. One of the ways Gregg took himself seriously was to carry his own bat bag, something today's players do all the time, but back in my day was a little unusual. It irritated a lot of our veterans, who as it was didn't care for the way management was trying to coddle Gregg and shoehorn him into a spot on the field, to where his at-bats would be siphoned from somebody else's stat line. Gregg could play short, second, or third, and he could play the corner outfield spots, but there was no room at the inn, with our crowded lineup. And it's not like he could play any of those spots so spectacularly well that we'd be a better defensive team with him in that position, and it didn't much matter to this arrogant, confident group of tight-knit veterans how highly touted Gregg Jefferies was as a hitter until he actually showed us something at the big league level.

Clearly, there was a good deal of stress and strain as Gregg tried to make a place for himself on the team. That's where the bats came in. A bunch of my teammates, who shall go nameless, rallied 'round a not-so-harmless prank suggested by one of our singular team-mates, who shall go named (Roger McDowell), who put it out there that we should saw Gregg's precious bats in half and put them back in his bag.

This seemed like a good idea to all concerned—all concerned, that is, except for Gregg Jefferies.

Got to admit, this was pretty funny, if you were aware of the tension that seemed to follow poor Gregg around our clubhouse like a black cloud, but let the record show that I had nothing to do with the bat desecration that followed. I *may* have known about it (emphasis added), but I was nowhere near the scene of the crime, and as I recall I even tried to stay away from the moment of discovery. It was only later that I heard about Gregg's furious reaction (which I had on good authority was priceless), and the fallout that came the way of the suspected assailants (which was also not without cost, as I will soon explain). Still, I was somehow fingered as one of the assailants—one of the most embarrassing moments of my career. I was embarrassed because I was being made to answer for the awful mistreatment of a young player who was really just trying to find his way. The coaches asked me about it . . . reporters asked me about it . . . for whatever reason, it was generally assumed that I had a hand in it, and I hated how the thought must have made me look in the eyes of others.

The cutting of the bats, in a vacuum, wouldn't have been that big a deal, because they were easily replaced. No, it was what the bats symbolized to a kid like Gregg Jefferies. They were the tools of his trade, and here the leaders of this professional organization he was desperately trying to crack were not only keeping him from those tools, we were also destroying them. We were trying to break him down. You'll notice that I used the universal *we* in those last two sentences—not because I was directly involved, but because I was aware of this cruelty as it was going down and didn't do a damn thing to stop it.

Yeah, it was funny, but it was also harsh, vindictive, over-the-top, and I would have liked to think that we were all better than that—that *I* was better than that, at least.

Gregg Jefferies never forgot that Roger McDowell had been the mastermind of this episode, and a couple years later, after Roger had been traded to the Phillies, the friction between them led to a bench-clearing brawl. It was our last home game of the 1989 season, and Roger got Gregg to ground out to the right side of the infield to end the game. As Gregg was running to first, Roger was crossing from the mound, shouting at him. I couldn't hear what he was shouting, but Gregg surely could, because as soon as he touched the bag and the game was ended he spun on his heels and darted back toward Roger, like a bull charging a toreador. He lowered his head and barreled into him, and the two started going at it, hard and heavy.

If you go back and look at the footage from that game, you can hear the Mets' legendary broadcaster, Ralph Kiner, in the booth, lending a kind of poetic headline to the proceedings:

He said, "Teammates once. Enemies now."

Ralph didn't know the half of it, I don't think, but what's interesting to me now in the retelling is the way the situation had flipped. When Gregg came up, those of us who should have known better looked the other way while he was razzed and tormented. Our thinking at the time was that Roger McDowell, his chief razzer-tormentor, was one of us. And now, Roger was in a Phillies uniform, and as much as we might have liked him, as much as the friendships we shared with him as individuals and as a team might have endured, he was in the other clubhouse. Gregg Jefferies was in a Mets uniform. He was in *our* clubhouse. And when he charged the mound and went at Roger, we fell in right behind him. We ran to the field from the dugout, from the bullpen and piled on. Because that's what teammates do, right? We treat you like shit, but it's okay because *we're* the ones treating you like shit. When our opponents treat you like shit, that's when we have a problem.

We had Gregg's back, at last.

On a personal note, I should mention that Gregg's Mets tenure outlasted my own. I was traded to the Expos during the 1991 season, while Gregg was still trying to establish himself and fulfill all that promise that went with all that high touting. Finally, at the end of the 1991 season, the Mets gave up on him, packaging Gregg with Kevin McReynolds and Keith Miller and shipping them all off to the Royals in exchange for Bret Saberhagen, just two seasons removed from his stunning Cy Young Award–winning season. It was one of the last truly blockbuster trades I can recall, and I mention it here for the way it bumps up against the Rick Honeycutt story I told a couple pages back. After all, it was Keith Miller who broke up the no-hitter I had going in Kansas City, before Rick came on and threw away the 1–0 lead I'd been nursing, which allows me to offer the dubious argument that were it not for this notorious bat-sawing incident, were it not for the struggles of Gregg Jefferies in a Mets uniform, and the decidedly negative energy that attached to his career in New York, that blockbuster Saberhagen trade might never have happened. Keith Miller might have still been playing for the Mets, or perhaps have been traded elsewhere, and he wouldn't have been in the lineup that night to hit that eighth-inning single and erase my no-hitter.

Here again, even in this circuitous way, it all ties in.

Stan Jefferson was one of two can't-miss prospects to emerge from the Mets' farm system who somehow missed.

Herm Winningham was the other. Understand, the can't-miss designation was mine. Understand, too, there's probably a reason why I never became a scout or a general manager or a judge of innate baseball talent other than my own, because neither one of these guys ended up with the career I'd imagined for them.

Stan was just a stunning talent, who roamed centerfield like he'd been born there. He'd grown up in Co-Op City, in the Bronx, came from a real rough-and-tumble background, was tough as nails. I used to watch him chase down fly balls and think, Man, this kid can play! He bounced around the bigs for a couple years, but never managed to put it all together, and after his career was over he became a New York City cop. In fact, he was on duty on September 11, 2001, and ended up working at Ground Zero following the collapse of the Twin Towers, so I guess his ultimate contribution to the life of our city came away from the ball field.

First time I saw Herm play was in Toledo, Ohio, when Darryl Strawberry got the call to the bigs and we brought Herm up to the Tides to replace him. I think he went five-for-five in his first game for us, with a double and triple and two stolen bases.

I looked on and thought, Fuck that Strawberry guy. This guy can *play*!

Herm Winningham ended up being a big part of another blockbuster trade—going to the Expos with Hubie Brooks, Mike Fitzgerald, and Floyd Youmans in the deal for Gary Carter. Hubie was the established star in that trade, while Herm was widely seen as the future star, but that big career never quite materialized.

Far and away, he was the most beautiful runner I've ever seen in a baseball uniform. Such a perfect gait! He should've been an Olympian—a 200-meter man, or a 400-meter man. Oh my goodness, that young man could fly.

· · ·

Doug Johns, the Oakland A's left-hander, and *Julio Valera,* the New York Mets right-hander, are inextricably linked in the story of my career—at least, they're linked in the story I tell myself of my career, and the story I tell myself is this: Doug Johns effectively put an end to my career in Oakland, while Julio Valera effectively put an end to my time in New York.

I'll tell Julio's slice of the story first, because that's how it came about. As a backdrop to Julio's appearance in my life and on the Mets roster, I'll note that from the time I was called up in September 1983, up until the last month of the 1990 season, I never spent any time on the disabled list. I took the ball every fifth day for seven full seasons—not a lot of pitchers can say that. However, there's a teeny-tiny asterisk I need to append to that claim, because I did miss my last couple starts of the 1987 season after pulling all the ligaments in my thumb in an ill-advised play at first base against the St. Louis Cardinals, after which a hand surgeon fixed me up and put me in a cast. I was done for the season, but I was never placed on the disabled list because the injury happened in the second week of September, and with our expanded roster there was no need for Mets management to sideline me . . . therefore, the asterisk.

I returned to form by the start of the 1988 season, and kept my self-styled streak going all the way to late in the 1990 season, and a game I might have started against the Pittsburgh Pirates at Three Rivers Stadium. The race for the top spot in the National League East was tight—we trailed the Pirates by two and a half games, headed into the final few weeks of the season, so this was a big game for us. A big game (potentially!) for me. But I'd started shuttling back and forth to the bullpen toward the end of August. My spot in the rotation was skipped a couple times, owing to rainouts and holes in our schedule (and, admittedly, to various fallings-short in my performance), so I came on in relief a time or two. The "demotion" to the bullpen, if that's what it was, was probably deserved. I'd struggled that season, was pitching to an ERA of around 5.00 for most of the year, but every time my turn came around in the rotation, I thought Davey would give me back the ball and I would fight my way back to whole.

This game against the Pirates had loomed on the calendar for weeks, and in the back of my mind I believed I'd get my shot, but it was not to be—and the reason it was not to be was because my manager and coaching staff thought the team had a better chance to win behind Julio Valera than they did behind me. And the reason they thought *that* was because I hadn't given them any reason to think otherwise.

I thought, *Julio Valera! How fucking bad am I that they're starting this chunky, out-of-shape kid ahead of me?* In a must-win situation? No disrespect to Julio, who'd done nothing but pitch his ass off to push himself into this conversation—but, at the same time, no disrespect to yours truly, who'd done nothing but pitch *my* ass off for the whole of my career, which may or may not have seen better days.

It was the first indication from Mets management that I wasn't figuring into their plans—and, got to say, I don't think I took the news all that well. I watched the game from the bullpen, and poor Julio got hammered, and I'd like to think I'm a good person and that I wasn't rooting for him to kick it—but then, here I am, all these years later, vengefully reporting his pitching line:

IP	H	BB	R	ER
2	8	2	5	4

I repeat, no disrespect to Julio—even as I'm disrespecting Julio. Somehow, I stuck around with the Mets through the start of the

1991 season, but this game in Pittsburgh marked the beginning of the end for me in a Mets uniform.

The beginning of the end for me in an A's uniform was also connected to the vainglorious pride I felt in never having been placed on the disabled list, asterisk or no. Here again, I was struggling. The 1995 season was winding down, and I was having trouble getting people out. In my own mind, for some reason, I chose to see this as a hiccup rather than a chronic condition. Throughout my career, I'd have a lousy start or two, but I was always given the ball and a chance to set things right. This time, though, I couldn't seem to get out of my own way. In what would turn out to be my last start for the A's—indeed, my last appearance on a major league mound—I gave up five earned runs in five and a third innings. In the start before that, I gave up three earned runs in five innings—a quality start in no one's estimation, especially mine.

Tony La Russa came to talk to me about it, as I most certainly knew he would, as I most certainly *feared* he would—although, to be honest, *feared* was not exactly the right word in this context. Perhaps it would be more accurate to say I *half-expected* it, with the other half falling into the *half-dreaded* column. Sure, I'd known the time would come when I would have to hang it up as a ballplayer. I could see that day approaching, even as I would have wanted to put it off and find a way to leave the game on my own terms, on some kind of high note. But I'd pitched myself and my manager into a tough spot, and it was the time of year when a going-nowhere team looks to its developing pool of players and starts thinking about next year, and all the years to come.

And so, Tony called me to his office—on my birthday, no less!—to recite his lines in the play that attaches to the life of every ballplayer, in one way or another, at one time or another. He said, "Ronnie, we're gonna start this kid Doug Johns. We're shutting you down for the rest of the season."

He was nice enough about it, professional enough about it . . . and yet there was something *about it* that rubbed me wrong. I mean, *Doug Johns*? I felt the same way I had when I was dropped from the rotation for Julio Valera. When you lose your job, you'd like it to be to a top prospect, at least. I'd seen these guys pitch. I could see there was a ceiling on what they'd achieve in the bigs. But the A's wanted to see what this kid could do, and it had been a while since I'd been able to impress the club with what *I* could do . . . so this was what it had come to.

We talked. It was a conversation I never wanted to have, but here it was. Tony laid it out for me, said he wanted me to stick around, thought I could be a helpful presence in the clubhouse, maybe drop some wisdom and game-won strategy on our young pitchers. It was a gratifying thing to hear, that he thought I could be of use as a mentor of sorts, but in order to do that the team would have to make some sort of move—meaning, I'd have to go on the disabled list. There would be no role for me coming out of the bullpen. The organization was crowded with young pitchers, and Tony wanted to give them a look. The roster wouldn't expand for another couple weeks, and the team (rightly) wanted to give my spot to someone who might be able to contribute in the future.

Tony was decent, and gracious, and kind. I was wounded, and stubborn, and proud. It had been a badge of honor to me that I'd never been on the disabled list, and I couldn't see signing on for a stint on the DL over some roster maneuvering. I wasn't hurt—I was just lousy, maybe even done.

I said, "You realize I've never been on the disabled list."

He shook his head—said, "I didn't know that."

I said, "You realize, too, that today's my birthday."

He shook his head—said, "I didn't know that, either. Tell me one of those things is wrong."

This time, I was the one shaking my head. I said, "Afraid not."

I thought back to one of the first meaningful conversations I ever had with Tony, about a month into the '92 season. The A's had traded for me in '91, and I'd yet to give the club any indication that they'd made a sound move, so he called me over one day after I'd been shagging flies during batting practice. We were in Detroit, and he came out to short center field to meet me.

He said, "Hey, Load. Got a minute?"

Yep, he called me Load—I guess because I was the opposite of a load, an easy guy to manage.

I said, "Sure, what's up?"

He asked how I was feeling, if there was something maybe going on at home.

Turned out, there was . . . and I said as much. My first wife and I would end up getting divorced years later, but we were going through some hard times and I mentioned to Tony that there was some tension between us.

He listened, let me finish, and then he turned and offered the best piece of advice I ever got from a manager. He said, "As a human being, I care. But as your manager, you've got to start winning some fucking games."

This was true enough, and for a while in there I was able to turn things around. I actually had some excellent years in Oakland, even pitched my way to a big contract . . . but now those excellent years seemed to be coming to an end, along with that big contract, and my time was up. In the end, I decided to swallow my stupid pride and accept that I'd be DFA'd—designated for assignment—because my other options were to force the team to release me, or to retire. I hated the idea of being released even more than I hated the idea of being disabled, and to retire meant I would forfeit that balance of my salary for the rest of the season—about $500,000.

I did the math, and weighed my options, and blamed the dilemma on the emergence of Doug Johns as a viable piece of the A's plans, same way I'd blamed my demotion from the Mets' rotation on the emergence of Julio Vargas. But it wasn't them! It was me! I was the bum, and I would have been shown the door either way.

Stupid pride, huh?

The most meaningful exchange I had with one of my teammates after a game? That would have to be the time **Ray Knight** wrapped me in one of his great big bear hugs at the end of an 11-inning nail-biter in St. Louis. It was October 1, 1985, and we were up against John Tudor, who was absolutely untouchable. He'd gone 1–7 to start the season, and was now sitting at 20–8—one of the greatest pitching runs in recent memory.

Tudor was untouchable on this night as well, shutting us out through 10 innings. Happily, I was a little untouchable as well, matching Tudor frame-for-frame through regulation, until Jesse Orosco took the ball from me in the 10th. Ken Dayley came on in relief of Tudor in the top of the 11th, and hung a 1–1 breaking ball to Darryl Strawberry, who broke the scoreless tie with a *ginormous* home run that hit the clock in the right field bleachers—one of the home runs Mets fans *still* talk about.

Jesse retired the Cardinals in the bottom of the 11th to preserve the victory, and after the game Ray Knight ran over to me in the clubhouse, animated as hell. I could see he'd been crying, with joy and emotion. I said, "You all right, buddy?"

He said, "R.J. We just won one of the biggest games we'll ever play!"

I guess he was right—it *was* a big win. It pulled us to within two games of St. Louis for National League East lead, with five games to play.

And he kept on—said, "If it wasn't for you, we wouldn't have had a shot."

By the way, like a lot of my teammates on those Mets teams of the 1980s, Ray called me R.J., a nickname I'd worn since I was a kid. As a "junior" to my father's "senior," I was known to friends and family as Ron Jr., or "R.J." The handle followed me to Shea, where I was grateful for the way it helped me distinguish between shout-outs from those who knew me and those who didn't. At the ballpark, if someone called out to me as "Ron" or "Ronnie" or "Darling," I knew it was a fan, or maybe a reporter, or someone I'd only just met. What's curious is that the name somehow traveled with me to Oakland, where my new team-mates didn't know me from Kirk Dressendorfer. And yet the name stuck all over again—thanks, in large part, to the shower shoes we all wore. Back then, ballplayers were in the habit of marking their shower shoes with their nicknames—a locker room version of the Players Weekend tradition started in 2017—and here I could only hope that as my new teammates were checking me out in the shower they were only looking at my shoes.

Getting back to that Ray Knight moment, I appreciated the comment, and the tears and the bear hug that came along with it, and as it turned out there was a little more aftermath to this outing. The next night, before the second game of the series, Dwight Gooden going up against Joaquin Andujar, Mets public relations director Jay Horwitz came over to my locker and told me some reporters wanted to speak to me. He'd set up a mini press confer-ence to handle the scrum. I must've made close to seventy starts in my big league career to this point, and no reporter had ever asked to interview me on the day *after* one of my appearances.

I went with Jay to the small press room and faced the cameras and microphones. It felt to me like there were a couple hundred reporters jammed in there, but in truth there were maybe twenty or thirty. The questions came flying from every direction:

How does it feel, to pitch such a big game?

Was it intimidating, to go up against John Tudor, with how well he's been pitching?

Any advice for Doc?

The underlying theme of the press conference was that the game the night before had been a kind of coming-out party for me. Davey Johnson had already held a press conference of his own, during which he allowed that I had somehow become a big league pitcher with those nine shutout innings against the Cardinals.

I heard that and thought, Wait, I thought I was *already* a major leaguer. WTF?

It's worth noting here that there had been some controversy to Davey's decision to start me in the first game of such a key series down the stretch. Doc had been having a lights-out season of his own in 1985—he was every bit as untouchable as John Tudor. In *his* press conference, Davey defended his decision, blowing just the right amount of smoke my way, saying how we wouldn't be in this position to challenge for the division without my performance on the mound. He also pointed out that with the first game of the series in the plus column for us, we now had Doc to come in behind me and pitch the second game.

"How great is *that*?" he said.

Pretty great. And, pretty great that a guy like Ray Knight was able to see the moment for what it was and take the time out of his postgame celebration to seek me out and offer his heartfelt comments—they meant the world to this kid pitcher, who some-how became a major leaguer that night, at long last.

I mentioned earlier that I arrived to the Mets with Walt Terrell in a trade for *Lee Mazzilli*, who has become one of my closest friends in the game over the years. Lee had had an incredible run with the Mets, during one of the team's fallow periods, when he emerged as the team's marquee player—he made the All-Star team in 1979, and was a beloved figure at Shea for the all-out way he played the game (and, a little bit, for his movie star good looks and the way his uniform seemed to fit him like it had been painted on his body).

Lee was the quintessential local boy made good, made a real con-nection with the fans, and when he was traded to the Texas Rang-ers for the likes of me and Walt, he famously asked a reporter who he'd been traded for. When the answer came back that he'd been traded for two pitchers nobody had ever heard of, he said, "What, I was traded for two minor leaguers?"

Like it was some kind of disgrace.

I didn't think it was so funny then. I do now.

I always thought *Roger McDowell* threw a spitter. He would never admit to it, though, and I never could get conclusive proof. Whatever he was throwing, whatever he wasn't, he managed to put together one of the all-time great seasons out of the bullpen in 1986. He ended up winning 14 games and saving another 22—an amaz-ing season.

If you go back and look at the numbers from that year, at the ways Davey Johnson used his bullpen, you realize that Roger and Jesse Orosco did most of the heavy lifting. Most teams had a core of seven or eight relievers they relied on, similar to today's game, but these were our go-to guys, in almost *any* situation. And our starting pitching had some serious length—at season's end, 1,259.1 of the team's 1,484 innings pitched were logged by Roger, Jesse, or our five primary starters. (That's almost 85 percent of our innings, for those of you who need help with the math—an unusually high number to be shared by just seven pitchers.)

If you'd have asked me back then if I thought Roger had the stuff to become one of the game's preeminent pitching coaches, I'd have looked at you funny. Roger was a goofy clubhouse presence. He wasn't *just* into fucking with our prima donna rookies and sawing their bats in half. He would also walk across the dugout or clubhouse on his hands and fill his pants with baseballs. He would sneak up behind you and pull a *hot foot* move, or start a rally cap movement out in the bullpen or on the bench.

A good, good guy to have on your side when you went into battle—and a good, good guy to pick up your team when spirits were sagging.

Mark McGwire was the biggest person I ever played with. He once wrapped his forearm around my neck and head (as a form of greeting, I guess), and all I could think was, Oh my God, this giant is going to crush me with his forearm.

I remember that he was struggling when I joined the A's midway through the '91 season. He ended up hitting just .201 that year, his home runs were *way* down, but his disposition was cheerful, professional. A couple years later, about a month before I was unceremoniously retired by the A's, I saw him hit three home runs off Boston left-hander **Zane Smith** in a game at Fenway Park—one of the most amazing individual accomplishments I ever witnessed from the dugout.

I didn't know the first thing about steroids, and the only

performance-enhancing drugs I ever saw being passed around in a big league clubhouse were alcohol and amphetamines, so I have nothing to say on the question of whether Mark or his fellow "Bash Brother" Jose Canseco might have been juicing during their time in Oakland. All I know is that he was a tremendous teammate, with the resilience to bounce back from a dreadful season, and forearms that could have crushed a watermelon.

Or, me.

A word or two on the steroid culture that attached to the game during my playing days—at least, as I came to see it . . .

You have to realize, when I first started going to the gym at twelve and thirteen years old, to add a pound of muscle to get ready for the football season, there were no kid fitness facilities. There was no yoga, no Pilates, no personal trainers my parents could have hired by the hour to whip me into shape. (As if!) No, everyone from the fifty-something men trying to stay in shape to kids like myself, we all went to the same dank, stinky gym. We all went through pretty much the same motions. And yet it was in these shitty gyms that I first started to notice needles on the bathroom floors, in the trash bins, because you had everybody in there. You had body builders, and big, bruising football players hoping to get recruited into the college ranks. It was a strange atmosphere, and when I figured out what was going on it galled me that some of the older kids I was playing with and against in high school were somehow adding thirty pounds of muscle, while I was doing the very same workouts and could only add that single pound. I came to resent those guys with the perfect abs, pecs, triceps, biceps . . . but then I filed away that resentment and went about my routine.

I've written before about the drug use in the Mets clubhouse during my time there—but, again, as far as I could ever tell the substances that were being abused were limited to amphetamines and alcohol. In Oakland, things were different, and it took me a while to spark to those differences. Understand, I never actually saw any *evidence* of steroid use during my time in Oakland, like those left-behind needles in the gyms I used to go to as a kid, but there was *trace evidence* all around.

I'll explain: I'd always thought of baseball as a talent game—you know, that if you got big and strong and tight, if you weren't loose and limber, it would hurt your game at some point. You'd somehow mask your talent, keep your body from what it was naturally inclined to do. But what I had come to realize over time was that baseball was really a game of attrition. I can remember walking into clubhouses my entire career and seeing veteran ballplayers slumped in their locker, struggling to lift a cup of coffee. The effort was in getting back out there on that field, day after day. Hanging on, hanging in. Hoping to get just a couple more hits, make a couple more plays. If you were at 215 pounds to start the season, you might step off the scale at 197 pounds in the dog days of August, wondering how the hell you'll keep the weight on and finish out the season. And to finish it strong? Forget about it. But here in the Oakland clubhouse, there were guys moving around with the same energy they'd felt on Opening Day. They were at one hundred percent, all the time.

That should have been a tell. But it wasn't . . . not just yet.

There was a phrase you used to hear a lot in the game: *the best players are the ones who keep their dicks hard for six months.* That's a little crude, I know, but it gets right to the point. The greats of the game are the ones who find a way to play at full strength, full throttle . . . every single day. That's what steroids could do for you, I was made to realize once I got to Oakland. Like I said, I should have realized it straightaway, but I was a little slow to see what was right in front of me. Instead of slouching in their lockers after a game, my A's teammates would hit the gym for an hour, almost to a man. It took me a while to put two and two together on this, but there it was. And yet I never reached for those pills, those creams, those needles. Why? Well, in part because I'd always tried to conduct myself on and off the field in ways that would not embarrass my parents. That was a big driver for me—earning and keeping the respect of my family. If my father ever thought I cheated or took drugs to get better at baseball, it would have killed me.

Instead of FOMO (a fear of missing out), I had FOSMOM (a fear of shaming my old man), but alongside of that I was also naive. I stupidly thought that talent would prevail, over time. I believed that the natural way of playing the game, studying the game, honing *my* game would see me through. That's the line I'd been fed my entire baseball life, and in the end I thought that if you played the game *the right way,* the baseball gods would smile upon you. Success would find you, and it wouldn't come from a syringe or a bottle of pills or a tube of cream. It would come from sweat and effort and an unwavering belief in your own abilities and in the game itself.

What the hell did I know, right?

Kevin Mitchell was famous in the Mets clubhouse for cutting people's hair. I loved the guy, but I wasn't letting him anywhere near me with a pair of scissors.

He'd had a tough childhood, getting in and out of trouble, eventually bouncing from high school to high school in the San Diego area. He had a stepbrother who was killed in a gang-related incident. If it wasn't for baseball, or sports in general, Kevin used to say, he would have been dead or in jail.

That hardscrabble reputation followed him all the way to New York, where he seemed to love playing to his street kid image. At one point, there was a rumor running through our clubhouse that Kevin had decapitated his girlfriend's cat—a rumor that was later debunked by Dwight Gooden in his autobiography. I didn't know whether to buy Kevin's story at the time, but the Kevin Mitchell I knew wasn't like that. Yes, he'd had it tough, and he liked to talk a big game, but he was a gentle soul with a heart of gold. And he was an enormous talent. About the best thing you can say about that 1986 Mets team was that we were so good we couldn't even find a spot in the lineup for a guy who would go on to become a National League MVP. Gary Carter used to call him "World"—as in "All-World," a nod to the dynamic basketball player World B. Free—because he could play pretty much anywhere on the field, and do pretty much anything.

Once, when he was lighting it up as one of the best players in the game for the San Francisco Giants, Kevin made a barehanded catch in deep left field, off the bat of Ozzie Smith—a play that continues to get a lot of love on YouTube. But the barehanded catch I'll always remember came on the streets of Kenmore Square, just outside Fenway Park, immediately following Game 4 the 1986 World Series. My first wife, Toni, was mugged coming out of the stadium. She had a lot of money on her at the time—about $800, because we were headed to buy a new television set for my parents—and a couple thugs must have seen her flashing it at some point, because they tailed her and snatched her purse. Kevin took off after these assholes and managed to run them down—a genuine super-hero move on his part.

One of my favorite teammates of all time.

During my time in Oakland, we were visited in spring training by a fitness coach named Mack Newton, a Vietnam veteran. Mack was super-intense—you did not want to fuck around with this guy. He had us do this stretching routine that seemed to last for days and days. Really, it took just short of forever to get through his stretching ritual—probably a half hour or so, if you did it right.

(And if you didn't do it right, you would hear from Mack—better believe it!)

A lot of the guys took this routine pretty seriously. **Steve Onti-veros**, apparently, was one of them. Steve was a bit of a nut, and when Tony La Russa tapped him late in a game to pinch run, he started in on his stretching routine. La Russa was one of the first managers to regularly deploy one of his pitchers in a pinch-running role, on the theory that you don't want to waste a position player in a tough spot in a tight game if you've got a decent athlete on your staff who might do a serviceable job on the base path. Onto was certainly a decent athlete, to go along with his beautifully enig-matic personality, so he got the nod.

Now, most guys, when they're called on to pinch run, they'll maybe run up and down the line a couple times, stretch a little bit, and jog out to the field. But not Steve—he did the full Mack New-ton, before he was good and ready. It was an unusually long time before he ran out to the bag—at least ten minutes, a good long while for a garden-variety substitution.

Sure enough, the next batter hit a grounder to the shortstop, and Steve came up lame as he went into the bag at second, ended up pulling his hamstring.

I can't skate past **Jesse Orosco** on this alphabetical list of teammates without mentioning that it was Jesse who stood as the leader of the self-proclaimed "Scum Bunch" on those great Mets teams of the 1980s, which was primarily made up of Jesse,

Danny Heep, and Doug Sisk, and tasked with drinking as much beer as possible on our plane trips and bus rides.

Also, it was Jesse who stood up to Frank Howard at the end of the 1983 season, after our manager made another boneheaded move that left us players scratching our heads and challenging each other to say something to him.

Most of the guys were too chickenshit to stand up to Frank, even the wily veterans of our group, who knew their jobs were safe and that Frank's was somewhat less so.

Finally, the team seemed to turn to Jesse, and somebody said, "You talk to him. You're the only one who's having a good year."

Craig Paquette played some third base for us out in Oakland, and he'd go on to make a cameo appearance with the Mets later on in his eleven-year career.

I took him aside one day before a game against the Texas Rangers. Juan Gonzalez was in the middle of one of those stretches where you could just not get him out. He was like that, as a hitter, and it fell to us pitchers to look for a hole in his swing or some way to maybe throw some ice on his hot streak.

At this point in my career, I didn't have a whole lot of weapons at my disposal, so I had to rely on my head to get Gonzalez out, and my head was telling me that I could pitch him down and in.

I gave Craig a heads-up, because if I was pitching Gonzalez down and in that meant he would likely pull the ball on the ground.

I said, "Play as deep as you can, because he's going to hit that ball about a thousand miles an hour."

Craig nodded.

I said, "And play on the line, because he's going to pull it."

Craig nodded again.

That was how it was with "Juan Gone," during this one stretch. Even if you found a hole in his swing, he could still find a way to hurt you—like, *actually* hurt you.

Gonzalez followed the script and ended up driving two or three balls down the line at third, and Craig Paquette, playing deep, fielded them all flawlessly, like it was routine.

After the game, a group of us were sitting in the hotel bar, and talk turned to Craig and what a fine game he'd played. He'd had a big hit for us, too, so he was really one of the stars of the game. As we were talking, Craig happened to walk in, so we motioned for him to join us.

I was sitting with Tony La Russa and Doug Rader and a couple other coaches, because at that stage in my career I had more in common with the old guys on the team than I did with most of the young players.

I said, "Craig, that was some game you played today. Can I buy you a drink?"

He resisted at first—said, "No, no, I'm good." Because the last thing you wanted to do as a young player was to sit for a drink with the coaches and the wily veterans—it might've messed with your cred.

One of the coaches pressed him on it—said, "Goddamn it, kid. A game like that, you deserve a drink."

So Craig relented and turned to the bartender and ordered a piña colada.

Doug Rader heard that and pounded his fist on the bar—said, "You'll have a what?"

Craig sheepishly repeated his drink order—said, "I'll have a piña colada."

"The fuck you will," Doug Rader shot back. "What the fuck kind of drink is that? No major league ballplayer orders a piña colada."

Of course, this was the same Doug Rader who'd been a team-mate of Jim Bouton's on those rabble-rousing Houston Astros teams of the late 1960s, the same Doug Rader who was famously called out in *Ball Four* for taking a shit on a teammate's birthday cake, so when a guy like that tells you a piña colada is somehow beneath your station as a major league ballplayer, you turn tail and retreat from the bar without waiting for your drink to arrive.

Which was precisely what Craig Paquette did.

Alejandro Peña was a terrific Dominican pitcher who had a couple great years out of the bullpen for the Dodgers, the Mets, and the Braves, but I'll always remember him as the guy with the best clubhouse nickname. For some reason, we all called him "Dirty, Stinky, Rotten, Filthy Al Peña." I never knew why—he wasn't dirty, stinky, rotten, or filthy. But that's what we called him, in full.

And, best of all, he answered to it.

5

Some Crying in Baseball

Sometimes a ballplayer gets his legs cut out from under him before he gets a chance to find his footing. Or the bat taken out of his hands.

Case in point: ***Jose Oquendo***, who went on to have some excellent years for the St. Louis Cardinals, was a teammate of mine at Tidewater. He made it to the Mets at nineteen, didn't speak a whole lot of English, didn't really have a support system in place. It's hard enough making it to the bigs and fitting yourself in without having to deal with a language barrier, a cultural barrier, or any of a long list of barriers to keep you from feeling like you belong. He got his call-up ahead of mine, and had played most of the season with the Mets by the time I finally joined the club in September 1983.

Jose could play. To my eye, he looked like a young Ozzie Smith. A cannon for an arm. Soft hands. Excellent range. I wasn't the only one who saw his tremendous potential. He was a natural at short—a joy to watch, really. The knock on Jose, early on, was that he wasn't much of a hitter, and this was certainly true—but then, look at Ozzie's numbers from his first couple seasons. A lot of guys take a while to catch up to big league pitching, to figure some things out, and yet they still manage to keep their spot in the lineup because of their glove. And so it was with Jose. He was widely regarded as the Mets' shortstop of the future—and not by default, because there was no one better to assume the position. No, this was a kid with a sky-high ceiling, and I was only too happy to get to take the mound once again and have him playing behind me in the field. When you pitch for a living, it's a good and reassuring thing to know you've got guys behind you who can *play*.

Trouble was, Frank Howard was the manager of the present, and he was worried about his own future. We were at the butt end of another in a too-long string of miserable Mets seasons, and it was pretty clear to most people who followed the team that Davey Johnson was the manager of the future, but Frank was hanging on, digging in. He was one of those baseball lifers who needed to stay on in the game, whether for the money or the attendant fame or some combination of both. He was desperate to make a case for himself, determined to win ball games, and here we were, playing out the string, the dugout filled with September call-ups, while he was doing his impression of managing his ass off.

It was the bottom of the third, at Shea, and our guys were feeling *hitterish*. We had an early rally going. Jose had already taken a little bit of the steam from a second inning rally, when he came up with runners on first and third, nobody out, the Mets up 1–0 against Andy Hawkins and the San Diego Padres. Bob Bailor had singled in a run with an infield hit and immediately stole second, igniting a meager Sunday crowd of nine thousand. But then Jose struck out looking to take the shine off the inning, and we went into the bottom of the third up by that same 1–0 score. Here again, we got a bunch of people on base, batted all the way around to Jose in the eighth spot in the order, runners on first and second. Two outs. Two runs in. A chance, I guess, to get a meaningful start on what was an otherwise meaningless game. But a chance as well for Jose to maybe redeem himself a little bit, and fight his way out of another pressure-filled situation without a whole lot of actual pressure. This is how you shake the green from a young player; you put him through his sometimes-difficult paces and let him battle. You let him show you what he's got, or figure it out for himself. But that's not exactly how Frank Howard handled things in this particular spot. Instead, he sent in Rusty Staub to pinch hit. *In the bottom of the third inning!* It was a witless, heartless, gutless move on the manager's part, and everyone on the bench ached for Jose in just that moment. He was a good kid, enormously talented, and we all felt for him. The fans, too, sprinkled about the stadium, seemed a little stunned by the move.

Granted, Rusty was probably the game's premier pinch hitter at that time. He'd had an amazing '83 season for the Mets, and he'd go on to have an amazing '84 season, but he didn't belong in this game, bottom of the third. And, professional that he was, consummate teammate that he was, he knew it. But he grabbed a bat, stepped to the plate, and popped out to second base to end the inning.

In another world, on another team, that might have been that . . . except it wasn't, because the move left Jose Oquendo in tears. The poor kid was flattened, broken. I was sitting next to him on the bench when he was told he wasn't hitting, and he just started sobbing—like, a full-body sob. And ballplayers not being known as the most sympathetic bunch, you might think a kid like that, crying openly like that, would be laughed out of the dugout. But that's not what happened. What happened was that everyone on the bench that day, to a man, felt for this kid. It was unbelievable, unconscionable, the way Frank Howard *managed* this situation. I mean, I'd been a big league ballplayer for just a couple days—I'd yet to make my first start!—but even I could tell that this was not how things should go Really, it was the first time I'd seen something happen on a baseball field that I considered a tragedy, and in all my time as a player and now as a broadcaster and a lifelong follower of the game, nothing has come close.

And here's the killing part: I don't think Jose ever recovered from that moment. It shot his confidence all to hell. Somehow, he got it together after he was traded to St. Louis at the start of the '85 season, and his beautiful skills were finally realized and appreciated. And yet whatever was in him that made him special at nineteen years old, whatever sweet admixture of magic and talent had cast him as a future star, it was all erased on that afternoon at Shea Stadium. For no good reason. By a manager who appeared to be more interested in holding on to his job than in holding the hands of his young players.

Now, ballplayers aren't typically a demonstrative bunch. We show our support for a struggling teammate with a pat on the rump, a tap of a gloved hand against the leg—maybe, in extreme circumstances, a rub of the shoulder. We don't usually say very much, because we've got no idea what to say, other than "hang in there" or "shake it off" or "you'll get 'em next time." In the language of the game, these are the gestures and empty phrases we use to convey sympathy, to let our brothers know we're on their side, and here in the bottom of the third, at home, we took turns letting Jose Oquendo know we were with him.

And then, at the end of the third, after Rusty made the third out, we all kind of hung back and watched in silent sympathy as

Jose shuffled to the end of the bench and ducked into the narrow passageway to the team clubhouse. It was a walk of shame like no other. The way the dugouts were set up at Shea, you had to walk down four or five concrete steps and then turn a sharp corner, where there was a shitter off to the right. Then you had to walk up another set of steps, and along a dark, cave-like corridor that ran beneath the stands to the clubhouse entrance. It's a walk of shame most of us in that dugout would go on to make a couple dozen times in our careers, heads hung low, and then a couple dozen times more, and it would always suck. Always, always. And yet here, again to a man, I believe every one of us would have gladly traded places with Jose, if it would have chased the pain he was in over Frank Howard's inexplicable, inexcusable treatment.

W ho said there's no crying in baseball?

I can still close my eyes and picture **Wade Boggs** sitting in the Red Sox dugout after the final out of the 1986 World Series, looking out at our celebratory scrum, tears running down his face like there'd been a death in his family.

Now, it's possible I'm conflating the scene I took in with my own eyes that night on the field at Shea Stadium with the images I've collected on video highlight reels over the years, but I definitely looked over in that moment and saw Wade Boggs sitting dejectedly in the dugout, the very picture of disappointment and loss.

That had to be a tough one. The Sox had been up 2–0 in the Series. They'd had Game 6 in hand and could've won it all before the storybook rally that pushed Mookie Wilson's dribbler through Bill Buckner's legs. And they'd had their way with me in the opening frames of Game 7, jumping out to an early lead in the deciding game that eventually went our way. They'd been *so* close, in *so* many ways. And remember, this was long before the Red Sox organization went on that great winning run in the 2000s, erasing the "curse" that had haunted the team since the days of Babe Ruth, so they had the weight of their own history pressing down on them.

I felt for those guys in the Red Sox dugout, I really did. Maybe it's because I was a kid from New England, so even as I was yukking it up with my Mets teammates, feeling on top of the world, my heart was breaking a little bit for the team of my growing up, and somehow that heartbreak came into focus for me in that image of a teary Wade Boggs.

We were world champions by only the thinnest of margins. We'd barely won the World Series. But I found time in that moment to recognize that as good as it felt to come out on the winning end of things, that's how bad it felt to come up short. A guy like Boggs, who'd go on to become a world champion with the Yankees, had probably never experienced such a low moment as an athlete. He'd spent his life as a ballplayer on top of his game—that's how you get to the bigs, right? Sure, as a kid, you cry all the time when you lose a big game. I used to tell the parents on my kids' Little League teams that there were four certainties in youth baseball: one team wins, one team loses, one kid cries, and everyone wants to know where they're gonna eat after the game.

Don't know why, but every time I flash back to that wild rumpus on the mound after the game, where the weight of my piss-poor start was mercifully lifted and I was swept up in the joyful abandon of winning the World Series, I also see Wade Boggs, slumped over in the dugout, looking out at our celebration, biting back tears.

Those two images, in split-screen, are why we play the game— and why we keep coming back each spring to give it another go.

One of the most famous "crying in baseball" stories was also one of the most heartbreaking—and, heart-lifting. It happened during the 2015 season, as the trade deadline approached, and media outlets started reporting that **Wilmer Flores** and Zack Wheeler had been traded to the Milwaukee Brewers for center fielder Carlos Gomez.

Indeed, the reports started circulating *during* a game between the Mets and the San Diego Padres at Citi Field, a game that Wilmer Flores just happened to be playing. And, this being our electronic age, the trouble was compounded by the tweets and texts that quickly passed among fans-in-the-know like a contagion.

Soon, everyone in the ballpark seemed to know a trade was going down—everyone, that is, except for Wilmer Flores.

Typically, when a player is involved in a trade and a game is under way, the club will remove him from the game immediately. The big fear is a risk of injury, of course, but there are other compelling reasons for this—not least the prospect that once a player's allegiance has been shipped out of town, his effort and professionalism might tag along.

Here on this night, though, Wilmer and the Mets were going through the motions like it was business as usual. Word of the pending trade had reached us in the booth by this point, but the club had yet to make an announcement, so it was business as usual for us as well. We held our broadcasting tongues and waited on official word, even as the ballpark was fairly buzzing with the news. And yet when Wilmer stepped to the plate in the bottom of the seventh, the fans gave him a standing ovation—a tip-of-the-cap for his years of service. It would have been a fine and fitting send-off, except that Wilmer had no idea why the fans were standing and cheering. Who knows, maybe he thought they were trying to get a rally going, but then when he grounded out he got another Standing O—probably confused the hell out of him.

The fans cheered again when he took the field in the top of the eighth, except by this time Wilmer had picked up on the buzz. Someone on the bench or one of the fans must have said something to him, so now he was crying. Openly, unabashedly. He kept wiping the tears from his face with his bare hand—never realizing, I don't think, that our cameras were trained on him, highlighting his face-saving actions to viewers at home. There was even a shot of an intensely sad and nakedly vulnerable Wilmer, wiping at his tears, on the big screen out in center field, magnifying the weirdness and emotion and uncertainty of this scene *way* beyond the ways it might have played out in an earlier time.

Up in the booth, I was struck by the humanity of the moment. Yes, baseball is a business. Yes, players get traded all the time— often, out of a happy clubhouse into a miserable one. But what gets lost in the transaction is the fact that a player like Wilmer had been with the Mets organization since he was sixteen years old. This was the only team he'd ever known, the only uniform he'd ever worn— the players, the coaches, the fans, the front office . . . this was his American family. It would have been like me leaving home at sixteen, headed to make my mark in Venezuela, a place where I didn't know the language, didn't know a soul, and then having the rug pulled out beneath whatever place I'd managed to make for myself . . . just, *because.*

So I ached for this kid—I truly did.

Eventually, Ruben Tejada pinch hit for Wilmer in the bottom of the ninth, and by now we were talking about it in the booth—it had become the story of the game!—but for a couple innings in there Wilmer was in a kind of no-man's-land, a dead man walking, while the Mets front office was only postponing the inevitable.

Mets manager Terry Collins, to his great credit, later told reporters that he'd never received word from the club that Wilmer had been traded, and he only removed him from the lineup when the speculation became a distraction.

The great kicker to this story came after the game. Actually, there were *two* great kickers. The first was that the trade fell apart, on concerns over Carlos Gomez's back. Those fans-in-the-know didn't know so much, it turned out, and neither did the trigger-happy reporters who'd been out in front on this story. Wilmer was returned to the fold. It was like the trade never happened—which, in fact, was the case. It was never announced through formal channels, just rumored and buzzed and tweeted about until Wilmer Flores was reduced to tears.

(The moral of the story? Always wait for the physical.)

The second kicker came two nights later, following an off day, in another home game, this one against the Washington Nationals. The score was tied 1–1. Wilmer stepped to the plate to lead off the 12th inning and drove a 1–1 pitch over the fence in left-center for a walk-off home run, and as he rounded the bases Met fans went a little bit crazy. Check that: they went *a lot of bit* crazy. As much as they had been pulling for Wilmer the night of the near-trade, that's how hard they were cheering for him in these extra innings. And Wilmer drank it all in; he started pounding on the Mets lettering on his uniform as he jumped on home plate, becoming a kind of folk hero with that one swing of the bat—not because the game meant all that much on the long string of the season, although the Mets and the Nationals were *kinda, sorta* battling it out for the top spot in the division. No, the magic in that moment was redemptive. Wilmer had showed himself to be vulnerable, and human, and now that he'd bounced back from that low personal moment to hit a game-winning home run *in the very next game . . .* well, that gave the whole episode a storybook twist.

It was one of those rare times in my career as a broadcaster where

I was at a loss for words. In fact, there have been just two other times where what was happening on the field left me standing and cheering and unable to say anything but "Fuck, yeah!"—hardly the expletive of choice for a professional broadcaster, but I'm a card-carrying fan at heart. That I might have played the game for a stretch, and won a World Series, and offered color commentary to a couple thousand games doesn't shake me from who I am.

Those two other times? The first was **Johan Santana**'s 2012 no-hitter against the Cardinals—the first no-hitter in Mets history. As a former Mets pitcher, a member of a staff of aces that on any given night could have ended the team's albatross string of no no-no's, I knew as well as anyone in Citi Field that night what this meant to the team, to the city. A no-hitter is one of the game's singular accomplishments, and here it was damn near heroic, in today's terms, because Johan had thrown 122 pitches through eight, and there was all kinds of talk and speculation in our booth over whether or not manager Terry Collins would run him out to pitch the ninth. And so when Johan struck out David Freese on a 3–2 count to end the game and cement his place in New York Mets history, I stood in the booth and wanted to scream—"Fuck, yeah!"

Let the record show that Santana's no-no was one of the great moments in Mets history, and I have to think it was because it meant something to have the team's first no-hitter go to a stand-out pitcher. We've all seen memorable games thrown by forgettable pitchers, but Santana was anything but a no-name pitcher. He'd been one of the game's elite starters for almost ten years, so it meant that much more. I actually sought him out after the game and collected him in a big hug—the only time I've ever done *that* in my role as a broadcaster!

The other *Fuck, yeah!* moment came *after* the Wilmer Flores drama, in an unlikely moment offered up by the ageless wonder

Bartolo Colon, who himself had emerged as a kind of folk hero to Mets fans for the way he played the game with such joy. "Big Sexy" wasn't known as much of a hitter, though, having played most of his career in the American League, and now that he was getting on in years, and carrying a few extra pounds from his peak playing days, his at-bats were often a comic adventure. And yet, during a game against the Padres at Petco Park in San Diego in May 2016, Bartolo Colon swung the bat like Babe Ruth and by some miracle drove a ball over the fence for his first career home run, at the grand old age of forty-two—and here again, I stood and cheered and thought, Fuck, yeah!

One of the things I love about calling baseball games are the moments where you find yourself in unchartered territory. When something happens on the field that I've never seen before, never even considered, it scares the plain shit out of me in the booth because I've got nothing to compare it to, no frame of reference for it. The *language* of the game doesn't cover what I'm seeing. And yet at the same time, it's also exciting as hell, because you're not following a familiar script and you get a chance to improvise . . . to *riff*. And so to see a kid like Wilmer Flores battle back from what had to have been the worst night of his professional career to carry his team on his back and win a ball game with one mighty swing . . . well, it was a rare and beautiful thing, even as it left me speechless.

All I could do was stand and cheer, cry a couple tears of joy, and try not to lose my job by screaming "Fuck, yeah!" into the microphone.

The most emotional I ever was as a ballplayer? It would have to be when my buddy **Ed Lynch** was traded to the Cubs in 1986. He'd been my best friend on the team since the day I came up—and to this day, we remain close. Eddie's gone on to do some big things with his life. He got his law degree from the University of Miami, became one of the game's top scouts, and was the general manager of the Cubs for a stretch. He's a very bright guy and we just seemed to click.

What a lot of Mets fans don't remember was that Eddie had a solid 1985 season for the Mets, but he made only one appearance in 1986 before going on the DL with torn cartilage in his knee—and with the core of talented young pitchers on that team, you did not want to step away from the mound for too, too long. It was that old Wally Pipp scenario writ large, only here you had five or six Lou Gehrigs lined up in the bullpen ready to push you from your post.

I'm mixing my baseball metaphors here, comparing pitchers to position players, and far be it from me as one of those bullpen arms to compare myself to Larrupin' Lou, but you get the idea. No, *this* was not *that*—but it was *like* that, a little, because while Eddie was out our starting rotation fell into place and the Mets decided he was no longer in their plans.

Frank Cashen, our general manager, called Eddie to his office to give him the news, and Eddie called me immediately after. He was shaken, and so was I. This was my third year in the bigs, so I'd seen teammates come and go, but this was really my first taste of how quickly things can change in baseball. It hit me on a professional level *and* on a personal level. The game can be cruel, when you're on the inside looking out. Sports in general can be cruel. Here it seemed especially harsh, because everyone in the organization believed we were on the cusp of something special. And maybe I'm biased, because Eddie and I were tight, but I really believed he could have helped our club. We needed his arm, his baseball smarts, his calming presence. We were a better team *with* Ed Lynch than we were *without* him.

Now, Eddie and I weren't the type to hug it out or share any kind of tender moment over such as this. Ballplayers back then weren't wired that way—they're still not, in fact. A fist pump or a pat on the back was about all you could expect as a show of emotion. But that didn't make Eddie's departure any less emotional. We might have been a team of professional athletes, a team assembled to win ball games, put fans in the seats, and sell official team merchandise, but we were also a group of caring, feeling human beings. People around the game talk all the time about the character of a ball club, the makeup of a big league clubhouse, and what they're really talking about are the personalities that come together to create a winning environment. You'd think, with all the emphasis on team chemistry and such, there'd be a little more weight assigned to the character of a ballplayer and the personal relationships that develop among players—but baseball is a business, at bottom, and I came out of this knowing that putting in any kind of effort or energy in forging personal relationships with my teammates was counterintuitive to the game itself.

The fact that the 1986 Mets would go on to win the World Series and become one of the most iconic teams in New York City sports history only made me feel Eddie's departure more keenly. He felt it, too. He once told me it was like waking up on Christmas morning and finding out you were living with some other family.

When you get traded or released, your standing changes in an instant. One moment, you are such a part of your team, and the next you are so *not* a part of that team. The suddenness, the immediacy, the finality . . . it can feel awful when you're on the inside of it. It can be so impersonal—like the stories you hear from the corporate world, when someone gets fired and is swiftly escorted from the building. Someone packs up their belongings and sends it on to them—that's how badly they don't want you around after they let you go.

They don't even want you to say good-bye.

On a selfish level, Eddie's departure changed my life away from the stadium. There were only four of us on that team living in Manhattan at the time—Eddie, Keith Hernandez, Danny Heep, and myself. We had our own little fraternity within the larger Mets fraternity. After every Sunday day game, we'd go to Tokubei on the Upper East Side and eat sushi until we couldn't breathe, and at some point we'd spill out onto Second Avenue and Keith would do his Mendy Rudolph impersonation in the middle of the street, and we would be doubled up laughing and counting our many blessings and moving about like veritable princes of the city.

It was a good and meaningful time, inside a good and meaningful time, and Eddie was a key part of that. He was my teammate, my running mate, my hanging-out mate. He was my friend. We were inseparable. And, just like that, he was gone.

Best I can recall, there was only one time I cried on a baseball field during the run of play. I was fourteen years old, struggling through my first year of American Legion ball, alongside mostly high school players, with a couple college kids thrown into the mix. I'd played in Senior Little League at thirteen, my first time playing on a full-size field, with 90-foot bases, but I didn't really have the arm strength just yet for the big diamond. I could field, and I could hit, but I couldn't really get enough hop on the throw from shortstop, which had always been my position.

At fourteen, I'd aged out of the Senior league, so there was really no place else for me to play, and my American Legion manager decided he'd hide my young arm at second base. I wasn't too happy with that, but I made the adjustment. There were adjustments all around, that first year. I'd always been the best player on my team, the best player in the league, and now I wasn't. I'd always been able to dominate, and now I couldn't. Plus, now I had to learn to turn the double play from the other side of the bag—and this was where those tears came in.

There was a grounder to the left side of the infield, so I crossed to the bag to receive the throw, my back to the runner from first barreling into second. This was a big dude from one of the local colleges, and he played the game hard, like it mattered. He took me out—like, *out*. I look back on it now and wonder if it was a clean play or a dirty play, but then I remember that when I was a kid there was no such thing as a dirty play. Whatever it was, this college kid cleaned my clock. It ended up, I held on to the ball, but couldn't make the throw to first, and as I stood and dusted myself off I started choking back tears—not because I didn't turn the double play, but because I was so shaken up. I hurt all over.

You know how when you're a kid and tears start to well up and you're trying your darndest not to cry but there's nothing you can do to keep from crying? Well, this was one of those moments, so I immediately tried to cover my tears with the more acceptable tics and gestures of the game. I dabbed my eyes with wrist band. I took off my hat and rubbed my brow. I slapped my glove against my thigh, to distract me from the pain I was feeling almost everywhere else.

At the end of the inning, I remember jogging back to the dugout thinking, Holy shit, Ronnie, you better not let anyone see you've been crying. But, of course, everyone could see I'd been crying. They'd all assumed as much, I guess—I mean, I was a kid, playing with young men. They'd all seen me get the shit kicked out of me on that slide.

But nobody said anything. I sat by myself in that dugout,

embarrassed as hell, and vowed that I would never again let my feelings show on a ball field. Didn't matter if I was hurt, or sad, or wronged . . . I would file my emotions away for later.

And I nearly made good on my vow, except for one time, early on in my professional career, before I'd even made it to the bigs. I'd already been traded from the Texas Rangers organization to the New York Mets. I'd already spent a season in Tidewater—in my day, the Mets' Triple-A home. My ERA was solid . . . my won-loss record, not so much. And then our season ended, and a bunch of my Tidewater teammates were getting called up to play out the string with the big club. It was a little bit of a slap in the face, not to be called up, because the Mets were going nowhere. They needed a pitcher. I thought, *Gee, I must really suck.* I thought, *This is fucking bullshit.*

Steve Schryver, the team's director of minor league operations, took me aside one day in the parking lot to check in with me on this, see how I was doing. It was really great of him, and he said all the right things—said, "Hey, Ron. It's just not your time, but your time will come. Just keep working hard." He couldn't have been nicer or more understanding about it, but I couldn't hear it at the time. All I heard was that I wasn't getting called up, and I became emotional. I started to cry, right there in the parking lot, right in front of Steve—like a big baby. Oh my God, I was so embarrassed, so unprofessional.

So I doubled down on that promise I'd made to myself in my first year of American Legion ball, to keep my emotions to myself. Because, in the end, there might be crying in baseball, but there is no crying in baseball.

6

"Q" Is for "Quirk"

Jamie Quirk was one of my favorite targets as a catcher—an infrequent one, but a favorite just the same. We played together for a couple seasons in Oakland, and he was so earnest and interested in the particulars of the game I found him to be one of my most endearing teammates. I used to love pitching to him. He played with such joy, like it was a blessing for him to be on the field. He'd come to the ballpark early whenever he was due to catch. If it was an afternoon game, he'd be in the clubhouse, fully dressed, by seven or eight o'clock in the morning. Really. For a night game, he'd be good to go by noon. Also, really. He was just so happy to be in the lineup, to be called on to contribute . . . it's like he couldn't wait for the game to start.

He was my catcher one day, at home, for an afternoon game against the Blue Jays. He was there early, of course, greeted me like a puppy when I arrived an hour or so after him—like I said, endearing as hell.

After my warm-up, we went over our signs, which were always the same: one finger for a fastball, two for a curve, three for a slider. If he wiggled a finger, that meant he was calling for the change. I didn't throw a slider, so that left only the one, the two, and the wiggle, so there was not a whole lot of ground for us to cover. And not a whole lot of subterfuge to our system—to be sure, if the New England Patriots scouting staff was in the stands that day, they would have had no trouble stealing our signs.

I came out firing that afternoon. Everything was working. The Blue Jays hitters couldn't figure me out, and I was feeling it—just one of those days, you know. Every pitch Jamie called was the perfect pitch, in the perfect spot, and by some divine alchemy delivered by the Bay Area baseball gods, I was executing perfectly.

Every once in a while it happens that a pitcher and his catcher are so totally in sync that it starts to feel like they're playing the game at a whole other level. They're in a zone, dialed-in. The opposing hitters, even your own teammates, fade into the background, and it's just the two of you, playing catch, telling the ball what you want it to do. That's what it was like between me and Jamie on this afternoon at Oakland-Alameda County Coliseum.

He could've called anything.

At some point, late in the game, the A's up 6–0 and me about to face a couple future Hall of Famers in the Toronto lineup for the fourth time that day, he did. Jamie put down *two* fingers and gave them a little wiggle—a sign I'd never seen. If I'd stopped to think about it, I would have had no idea what pitch he was calling for, but there was no thought in what I was doing. I was just doing. If Jamie had stopped to think about it, he might never have flashed that two-finger wiggle. But for that one game at least, the two of us were hardwired to each other in this weird and wonderful way. There was no reason to think.

Instinctively, I knew Jamie wanted me to throw a slow curveball—like a changeup, with a twist. So I threw it. A couple batters later, he dropped the same sign, so I threw it again.

After the inning, I went over to him and said, "That's what you wanted, right?"

He said, "Absolutely."

I said, "I've never seen that sign before."

He said, "I've never given that sign before."

And it was like that. Synchronicity, of a kind.

The most unfortunate injury I ever saw on the field? That would have to be the time **Carlos Reyes** was given a spot start for the A's, pulled a butt muscle on his first warm-up pitch, and had to be ferried to the clubhouse on a stretcher.

The most amusing aftermath to a most unfortunate injury?

That would have to be the daily butt-rubbings administered to Carlos by my good friend Barry Weinberg, the A's trainer, who'd try to get the job done before the clubhouse started to fill with pre-game activity. I was closer to Barry than I was to a lot of my A's teammates, so I used to like to bust his chops. For a trainer, he was a little squeamish about this type of inappropriate touching, so I'd make an effort during the two or three weeks Carlos was rehabbing to get to the ballpark early. I lived by the stadium in those days, so it was nothing for me to wander by when Barry thought the place would be empty—basically, to annoy him. He'd look up from what he was doing and catch me ogling as he furiously rubbed Carlos's right butt cheek.

I'd smile and say, "Hey, Barry. How's it going today?" Trying not to laugh.

Barry would roll his eyes and say, "Fuck you, R.J."

And so it went.

L ike Roger McDowell, **Dave Righetti** wasn't someone I would have pegged as a future pitching coach or any kind of sage of the game. He was a loose, loopy presence in the clubhouse—probably one of the funniest guys I ever played with, and certainly one of the most fun. He had a head for the game, was a tremendous communicator, but he was also a bit of a nut.

He showed up at spring training in 1994, and I was surprised to see him. In those days, the news of the day and the front office maneuverings of our team didn't show up in our phones—our phones were still dumb. We didn't know shit, until it was right there in front of us—and now, right there in front of me, in Oakland A's gear, was Dave Righetti.

I said, "Rags, what are you doing here in camp?"

We'd known each other from our dovetailing careers in New York, when he was toiling up in the Bronx for the Yankees and I was out in Queens with the Mets. That's one of the curious side benefits to playing professional ball in a two-team city—you're connected to your counterparts on the other team like cousins. You wind up drinking in the same bars, attending the same fundraisers, moving in the same circles. I was only too happy to see that in the Venn diagram of the game our circles might overlap yet again.

He said, "I'm making the team." Like it was a done deal.

We got to talking, and I asked him why he was still playing. He'd been in the bigs for fourteen years, had made a bunch of money, had just finished a three-year run with the Giants. He'd truly had a remarkable pitching career. He was the first pitcher to throw a no-hitter and then to lead the league in saves—a feat that was matched by my friend and teammate Dennis Eckersley and, years later, by Derek Lowe.

I said, "You'd think, a guy like you, it's time to hang it up."

He said, "*Jim Deshaies*."

That's all—just "Jim Deshaies." Like I was supposed to figure out what the hell Jim Deshaies had to do with any of this.

I waited for the rest of it, and here it was: "If that fucking Jim Deshaies is still playing, then I'm still playing." Beat. "If he can find a team, I can find a team."

Just to be clear, Jim Deshaies had been a lights-out pitcher for a stretch for the Houston Astros. In 1986, he set a major league record by striking out the first eight batters to face him in a game, against the Dodgers—a record the Mets' *Jacob deGrom* would match twenty-eight years later, against the Marlins. At the end of that same 1986 season, Deshaies was famously left off the Astros' postseason roster, which I've always believed played to the Mets' advantage in the League Championship Series that year. He was a tough left-hander, always seemed to have our number, and with the way he'd been pitching he would have been a weapon out of the bullpen against some of the big left-handed bats in our lineup. And now here he was, all these years later, fighting for a spot on a big league roster, in a way that left Dave Righetti fighting to keep it going in his own career.

Rags was funny that way. He told elaborate, *you had to be there*-type stories, mostly about his time with the wild "Bronx Zoo"-ish Yankees of the early 1980s. One of the great traditions on that team, according to Rags, was the "beach club" he ran on road trips with fellow pitcher Bob Shirley. One guy was in charge of making sure there were enough shorts and bikinis for the invited guests. Another guy was in charge of collecting all the sand from those heavy, stand-up ashtrays you used to find by the elevators and in hotel lobbies. And then someone else was tasked with hauling a couple potted plants from the lobby to decorate the room upstairs. They'd spread the sand on the floor, set up the plants, and hand out the beachwear, and—presto!—it was Spring Break in downtown Cleveland, or wherever.

The sand on the floor just outside the room was key, because when the local talent came up from the hotel bar downstairs, that's how they knew where to find the party.

"We just told 'em we'd see 'em at the beach," Rags explained.

Joe Sambito came on to mop up during one of the most lopsided losses in Mets history—a night game in June 1985 against a nothing-special Phillies team.

It was just one of those games—a blowout laugher that can reveal a lot about a team's character, on either side of the score, and here we learned more than we cared to know about our teammate **Calvin Schiraldi**, who would leave our ranks in the off-season in the trade that brought Bobby Ojeda from the Red Sox to the Mets. You could make the argument, as I will be doing here, that Schiraldi's comportment in this nightmare '85 game against the Phillies might have cost the Red Sox the '86 World Series.

Here's what happened: Von Hayes led off the bottom of the first for the Phillies with a home run off Mets starter **Tom Gorman** . . . and it was downhill from there. Tom had gotten the spot start, and he'd been all excited because he would get to swing the bat—something our relievers didn't get much of a chance to do.

The thing about Tom was that he liked to talk. A lot. He wouldn't talk about himself in the third person, like Deion Sanders, but his funny confidence even spilled over to skills at the plate. To hear him tell it, he might just have been the best hitting pitcher since

Babe Ruth. He'd played at Gonzaga, and he'd go on and on about his exploits at the plate in college, telling us (a little too loudly) that he'd once hit two home runs in a game. Truth be told, most everyone in the Mets clubhouse who'd played college ball had hit two home runs in a game, including yours truly, but we never called him on it. We just let him blow his smoke, because that's how he was. It was hilarious to watch.

We called him Gorfax. I think he took it as a compliment, and none of us were inclined to correct his thinking.

Before the game that night in Philadelphia, Gorfax sat on the bench, tapping his bat, working the grip, putting it out there that he was going to do some damage at the plate. We should have known we were in for a rough night because he seemed to care more about his at-bats than he did about his spot start, and sure enough he never got to take his licks because he didn't make it out of the first inning. Davey Johnson pulled him from the game with the bases loaded, one out, and three runs already in.

Schiraldi came on and hit the next batter, and then gave up a grand slam to Von Hayes. (That's two home runs in the first inning for Von Hayes, for those of you keeping score at home.) We eventually got out of the inning, but Schiraldi got lit up again in the second, giving up a triple, three doubles, and four singles, although to his great credit he did manage to keep Von Hayes in the park and to *very nearly* get out of the second inning.

Now, this was where all that character business came in, because when a game gets out of hand there's a tendency among those players who aren't actually *in* the game to get a little loosey-goosey in the dugout. Talk turns to which position players might be called on to pitch, because of course you don't want to waste a legit arm in one of these situations. But when you're out there on the field, you're expected to give it your all—and when you're on the mound especially, you're meant to keep pounding the strike zone. There's a professionalism you want to see from your teammates, especially when you're taking a beating.

I didn't see that out of Calvin Schiraldi on this grim, laughable night in Philadelphia. None of us did. There was a *give-up* in him that came through in his body language, in his effort, in the look on his face that told us he wanted to be anyplace in the world but out there on that mound. Coming out of this one game, and handing the ball over to Doug Sisk with our guys trailing 16–0 in the bottom of the second, we all started to see Schiraldi as a losing player. Whatever respect we might have had for him going into this game was shot. And it wasn't just the players who noticed it—team management saw it, too.

He was pretty much done as a Met after this shit outing, and he finished out the season with us as a kind of clubhouse pariah.

Sisk managed to keep the Phillies off the scoreboard for the next couple innings, but then Joe Sambito came on and didn't fare much better than Gorfax or Schiraldi. Unlike poor Calvin, though, Joe took his lumps like a man. It was a thankless spot, in a game that had been lost in the first inning, so nobody begrudged a guy like Joe his shellacking.

We begrudged the hell out of Calvin Schiraldi, though. And it came back to bite him in a big-time way, because when he donned his Red Sox cap and came on to face us in the bottom of the eighth, Game 6 of the 1986 World Series—Boston up 3–2 in the Series, and 3–2 on the scoreboard—we all remembered the quit he showed in that Philadelphia game. Really, it felt to us like Red Sox manager John McNamara was waving the white flag and giving up on this game—no one on our side of the field feared Calvin Schiraldi. We didn't believe in him as a teammate, and he gave us absolutely no cause for concern as an opponent. Indeed, we were giddy at the thought of facing him. We knew we would get to him, and we did. We pushed across the tying run in the eighth on a Gary Carter sac fly with the bases loaded, and it was Schiraldi who set the merry-go-round in motion for us in the bottom of the 10th, giving up a couple singles and a wild pitch and the game-winner off the bat of Mookie Wilson that found its way through Bill Buckner's legs and into Mets lore.

And then, after kicking Schiraldi's ass in Game 6, we were feeling even more confident that we would kick his ass again in Game 7, and McNamara gifted us the chance to do so when he brought him in with the game tied in the bottom of the seventh.

We'd gotten a whiff of the stink of weakness on Calvin Schiraldi as he kind of shrugged his shoulders and went through the motions during that laugher against the Phillies, and now here we were a little over a full year later, in a series of games that mattered most of all, and we could still smell it on him.

When I was traded to Oakland in the middle of the 1991 season, the A's sent right-hander **Joe Slusarski** to their Triple-A team in Tacoma to make room for me on the roster—just one example of the dominoes that fall when a team makes a move. Joe had been up and down with the big club, but he seemed to figure in the team's plans for the future, so I think he took this demotion in stride. The assignment was only temporary: Joe was named to the A's starting rotation the following year, after beating out Jim Deshaies in a heated spring training battle for the final spot.

(Take that, Dave Righetti!)

Joe continued to pitch well and appeared to be on the upward arc of a solid career . . . until he wasn't. Before we broke camp the following spring, he played a round of golf with fellow pitchers

Gene Nelson and Rick Honeycutt at a resort in Scottsdale, where he was felled by a jumping cholla. Joe hit a ball into what passes for "rough" out there in the desert, where it came to rest near a bush or a cactus of some kind. It turned out to be a jumping cholla plant, which drops all these menacing stems and seeds to the ground at the slightest touch. Those suckers can be deadly! Joe got a mess of spines stuck in his pitching hand when he reached for his golf ball, and within minutes he was screaming in pain. His fingers swelled to the size of ballpark franks, and there was damage to the tendons in his middle finger.

He was never the same pitcher after that—at least, not in the eyes of A's management. He made two more appearances in an A's uniform, the first in relief of me in a game at Comiskey Park later that season, where neither one of us pitched well, even though we eked out a 12–11 win with a three-run rally in the ninth.

Joe finished out his career with the Astros and Braves, who (mercifully, for Joe) played their spring training games far away from the not-so-friendly confines of the Cactus League.

As I look over the names of my former teammates, I stop and smile when I get to **Rusty Staub**, who died on Opening Day of the 2018 baseball season, after a long illness.

I shed a couple tears, too.

I went to visit Rusty at the hospital in West Palm Beach during spring training, and it broke my heart to see him suffer. It breaks my heart, now, to think of him gone. Really, I can't imagine a world without Rusty in it—just as I can't imagine my career without him. Someday, I'll write a book about Rusty, who was such an influential part of those great Mets teams of the 1980s. He was also a huge influence on me. Remember, Rusty's career dates to 1961, when he was drafted and signed by the expansion Houston Colt 45's, the same year the New York Metropolitans opened for business. He later became an original member of the expansion Montreal Expos, where he starred for several years, and was embraced by the team's French-Canadian fans, who dubbed him "Le Grande Orange." He ended up playing for twenty-three years—the only player in major league history to collect at least 500 hits for four different teams.

Consider the baseball history baked into Rusty's career: his first year in Houston, he played with Pete Rennels, who'd had some big years in the 1950s and '60s for the Washington Senators and my beloved Red Sox. Rennels's first big league manager was Bucky Harris, who played with Hall of Famers like Walter Johnson, Goose Goslin, Charlie Gehringer, and Heinie Manush (another one of the game's all-time great names—the Tucker Ashford of his day!—and a helluva hitter), so I came to look at Rusty as a link to the game's rich and storied past.

My goodness, it was through Rusty that *I* was connected to these all-time greats as well, in a once-more-removed way.

Consider, too, the noblesse oblige that Rusty showed throughout his career. He was celebrated in our clubhouse for the annual picnic he held to raise money for the widows and orphans of New York City firefighters and police officers—an event that became even more important in Rusty's retirement following the tragedy of September 11, 2001. His extra efforts on behalf of those in need were an inspiration that left me thinking early on of the ways I could give back to the community once I became more established as a ballplayer—a model that continues to inspire.

For a kid like me, eager to soak up what I could of baseball tradition, and to learn the history of the tension that existed between Major League Baseball and the players' union—an issue that was very much at the forefront when I signed my first professional contract during the strike-shortened 1981 season—I could think of no better teacher than Rusty.

He was my friend, my mentor—a docent who helped to set the tone (and, the standard!) for my own lifetime in the game.

I only got to see Rusty play at the end of his truly remarkable career. By the time I joined the club at the end of the 1983 season, he was getting up there in baseball years. He was a little out of shape, but still a prolific pinch hitter—the best in the game at the time. And yet he didn't sign on for that role, with his second go-round with the Mets. When he rejoined the team as a free agent ahead of the 1981 season, Frank Cashen assured him he would be the everyday first baseman. At the very least, Rusty expected to be in the starting lineup against right-handers. But then the Mets went out and traded for Dave Kingman, bringing the one-dimensional slugger back into the fold for a second stint of his own, and Rusty was pushed from the starting lineup and relegated to the bench. Like the professional he was, Rusty never carped about the change to his circumstance, and I think he came to relish his role as the team's elder statesman.

Being around Rusty was like hanging with the Dalai Lama. His deep affection for the game, his deep well of understanding of the game's many nuances, his deep knowledge of the game's history . . . it was all there for a kid like me to absorb in full. You know how golfers talk so reverently about Harvey Penick as one of the great sages of *their* game? How his *Little Red Book* is considered a bible for golfers? Well, Rusty was like that for us players, only we got to soak up his hard-won wisdom and insights directly.

Rusty had all the answers, and he gave them to you straight. No bullshit, no sugarcoating. Once, he took issue with a slow curveball I threw to Mike Schmidt in a game against the Phillies. Never mind that I got away with the pitch—Schmidt hit a ground ball to short to end the inning. Rusty still had something to say about my pitch selection, and he had a special way of making his point. He came over to where I was sitting in the dugout and whacked me on the shin with a bat—not hard enough to leave a bruise, but hard enough to hurt. In the middle of a game!

I turned to him and said, "What the fuck, Rusty?"

He said, "Don't you ever throw a slow curveball to Mike Schmidt."

I wasn't really listening, and Rusty could see I wasn't really listening, so he elaborated—said, "Right-hander against right-hander. Power hitter. Do not ever throw a slow curveball."

I heard him, loud and clear—but the message didn't really sink in. I was too focused on the game I was still pitching.

Later that night, over sakes and beers at Tokubei on the Upper East Side, a couple blocks from Rusty's restaurant, I asked him what the hell he was talking about. One thing I want to make clear: Rusty wasn't the kind of guy who did idle chatter. He could bullshit with you as well as anyone, but when talk turned to the subtleties of the game he was all business. You knew you had to think long and hard before you pressed him on something, because you were talking to a true sage of the game, and you didn't want to waste his time.

I said, "When you whacked me on the shin, what was that about?"

He said, "I wanted to get your attention."

I said, "You have my attention. Why don't you throw a slow hook to a right-handed power hitter?"

He said, "Because they don't have to get it all. You could make a good pitch, and if they just get it out front, it's still a home run. You can beat them and they can still hurt you."

I thought, *Okay, good to know.* And I thought, *Could've done without getting whacked on the shin, though.*

The best example of Rusty's influence on our young ball club came about on the back of my desire to live in Manhattan during my rookie season. I'd joined the team as a September call-up in 1983, and made it a point to live in the city during the off-season, to try on the idea of being a bona fide New Yorker. What I didn't know at the time, however, was that the Mets had a strict policy forbidding rookies from living in Manhattan, so I got some push-back on this from Frank Cashen when I learned I'd made the Opening Day roster.

I had an apartment all lined up—a fully furnished one-bedroom sublet that belonged to this sweet old lady. The place was a great deal, if I could get past the sweet old lady furnishings. (If I was lucky enough to bring a girl back to the apartment, I realized, she would've thought I was living with my grandmother.)

Anyway, it was all arranged . . . until it wasn't.

Frank Cashen called me in to tell me about the team's policy, told me I would have to make another arrangement.

I happened to mention all this to Rusty, and he took it on himself to intervene on my behalf. He'd cast himself as a bit of an advocate for our young players—in part because he truly believed we needed a veteran voice to serve as a kind of go-between with management, but also because he loved to stick it to the owners. He'd had a contentious relationship with every front office he'd worked under, which was one of the big reasons he never stuck with any one club for too, too long. He was known to be a demanding player, at a time in the game when most players were still treated like chattel.

I didn't really appreciate any of this at the time, but I was nevertheless grateful for Rusty's help on this. He went up to Frank Cashen one day as we were preparing to break camp and made my case. He said, "Frank, this kid worked his ass off all winter. He's had a great spring training. He's gonna be a big part of this ball club. He's been living in the city the whole off-season, and I think you should bend the rules on this. I'll vouch for him. I'll make sure to drive him home with me every night, make sure he gets something to eat, makes sure he stays out of trouble."

To Rusty's great credit—and to my great surprise—Frank Cashen relented on this, and Rusty was good to his word, introducing me to life as a professional athlete in a city like New York and to the many charms of the city itself.

My career is inextricably linked to the career of **Frank Viola**, one of the dominant pitchers in the American League throughout the 1980s, who was traded from the Twins to the Mets in the middle of the 1990 season. As collegians, he and I faced off against each other in what many people have called the greatest college ball game ever pitched—that 1981 NCAA playoff game I mentioned early on in these pages, the one that pitted Frank's St. John's Redmen against my Yale Bulldogs.

Many have written about that game (including me in my first book, *The Complete Game*), but none so movingly or memorably as Roger Angell of *The New Yorker,* whose long-form account, "The Web of the Game," is widely seen as one of the small masterpieces of baseball journalism. That article, as much as the game itself, has helped to cement the game's place in college baseball history.

Someday I'll write about *that,* too, but for now I'll just offer up a thumbnail account, before turning to the story I want to tell about Frankie V: St. John's won the game 1–0 in 12 innings. Frank and I had been trading zeroes all game long. I was pitching a no-hitter through 11 innings, while Frank had merely kept us off the scoreboard with 11 shutout innings of his own. In the top of the 12th, I allowed a single to start the inning, and then the St. John's runner stole second, stole third, and came home on a double steal. In the bottom of the 12th, Frank gave way to a right-handed relief pitcher named Eric Stampfl, who was later drafted by the Mets and topped out with a season of Single-A ball at Lynchburg in the Carolina League. Stampfl finished us off, and that was it for us Bulldogs.

It was inevitable, then, that when Frank was traded to the Mets, folks in and around baseball would bring up this game. It was epic, historic . . . and Frank and I were at its center. Now that we were teammates, it was an opportunity to reflect on what it meant to pitch the game of our lives as our professional careers lay in wait.

So that's the backstory to our reunion with the Mets. The front story was that Frank Viola was immediately cast as the Rodney Dangerfield of our clubhouse. Certainly, he was given the least respect of any player with such impeccable baseball credentials: a former Cy Young Award winner, a former All-Star, a bona fide ace who would go on to win 20 games for the Mets in his first full year with the club. But with the Mets, in the words of Tom Petty, we kind of kicked him around some. We all called him "Half a Woman," a nickname repurposed from Frank's college career, pinned on him a second time by John Franco, his St. John's teammate. I suppose the name fit, because Frank wasn't exactly the best-looking guy on the team, and he certainly wasn't the biggest or the burliest.

Frank had already been tagged with one of the greatest baseball nicknames of all time by ESPN's Chris Berman: "Sweet Music." But to us, from almost the moment he set foot in Queens, he was known as "Half a Woman"—not exactly the most flattering moniker for a major league ballplayer, and yet Frank was such a good-natured soul who was so confident in his abilities as a pitcher that he never seemed to mind the ribbing he received off the mound.

To be honest, I was a little shocked to see my teammates ripping into him so mercilessly after he joined the club, but I joined in soon enough. I mean, he made himself an easy target, so why the hell not? Once, during his first full year with the Mets, as he was chasing his 20th win of the season, one of our teammates put a wad of chewing gum on the top of Frank's baseball cap as he went out to start the game. He pitched with that wad of gum on his cap for the entire first inning—a sequence that would have surely become one of the all-time great memes in today's social media age, but back then just induced a couple snickers from those who were in on it.

Bob Welch wrote candidly about his struggles with alcoholism in the book *Five O'Clock Comes Early*—one of the best baseball memoirs of all time. He'd had some tremendous years for the Dodgers, and had won a Cy Young Award for Oakland the year before I joined the team—going 27–6 with a 2.95 ERA.

He was one of the most unusual guys I played with in the bigs. He had a bunch of nervous habits, which today might be diagnosed as symptoms of ADHD, but back then were dismissed as peculiarities. Most peculiar, perhaps, was the way he would fidget before every start. He was so restless on the night before a game that he'd set off on a long walk, deep into the wee hours. It wasn't unusual for him to leave our hotel at eleven o'clock at night, if we were on the road, roam the streets of whatever city we happened to be in for a couple hours, and wander back at three or four in the morning.

It was the strangest thing. But that's what worked for him—it was a way to settle his nerves, I guess, and once you take alcohol out of the equation, you do what you have to do to stay the course and keep sober.

Now, contrast Bob's laudable coping mechanism with that of my friend Half a Woman Viola, who took a more typical approach. Like Bob, Frank would also get incredibly nervous before his starts, but since he wasn't an alcoholic he was able to drink to his heart's content to calm himself down—typically, two six-packs of beer the night before one of his starts.

Go figure.

I don't think I've ever been more ashamed of myself than I was on a bus ride early on in my Mets career, when I was over-heard making an off-color joke about **Mookie Wilson**'s ap-pearance. As bad luck would have it, the person who did the overhearing was Mookie, which of course explains the shame.

Now, out of respect for Mookie, I will not share the off-color joke here, but let the record show that it was not racist. It was simply insensitive, having to do with Mookie's looks, and I hated like hell that he'd heard it. Truth was, I'd always liked Mookie. I liked the way he played, and I liked the way he carried himself off the field. Over the years, connected as we are now by the threads of the game and the tapestry of Mets history, we've become good friends—like brothers, in a way.

Mookie was a class act, and I wasn't, and he stood from where he was sitting on the bus and walked back to my row. I could tell by the look on his face that he'd heard what I said. He did not look happy—and one thing about Mookie, if you ever watched him play or give an interview, he *always* looked happy.

He leaned into my seat and spoke to me privately—said, "Ron, I heard what you said. I expect more of you than that."

And that was that. He didn't wait for a response from me—just cut me with this respectful and altogether superior one-liner. Frankly, I was tongue-tied, couldn't have come up with the right thing to say if he'd given me the rest of the bus ride to think of it.

He walked back to the front of the bus and sat back down in his seat, leaving me to sit and stew in my embarrassment. Happily, mercifully, I found a way to apologize to him afterward, and many times since, and I offer yet another apology here in these pages.

Mookie was right, after all. I was better than that. And so was he.

For my last entry in this alphabetically themed portion of the book, I look to **Lewis Yocum**, a protégé of Frank Jobe, a pioneer of the Tommy John surgical procedure that has prolonged the careers of hundreds of major league ballplayers. Dr. Yocum was the West Coast orthopedic specialist working with Dr. Jobe, and he was also the team physician for the California Angels for a number of years.

I went in to see him early on in 1992, after I'd been rocked in back-to-back-to-back starts against the Twins, Indians, and Blue Jays—allowing five earned runs each time out, without ever making it through the fifth inning. Something wasn't right, and I was starting to think it was the beginning of the end for me as a pitcher. In golfer's terms, when I was traded from the Mets in the middle of the 1991 season, it felt to me like I was at the turn and headed for the back nine.

When you're an athlete—specifically, when you're an athlete who relies on his arm and a precision-tuned throwing motion that has been grooved into routine—you can tell when you're injured, when you're no longer the same. You don't need a diagnosis or a second opinion . . . and yet here I was, seeking a diagnosis and a second opinion, on the off chance that a medical professional might set me right.

I still had a couple holes I was meant to play.

Dr. Yocum sat me down on his examination table and reached for my elbow, played around with it a little. After about three hot seconds, he turned to me and said, "You have a serious issue here."

I nodded—said, "Tell me about it." With an attitude, you know.

Dr. Yocum was used to giving athletes difficult news, so he was patient with me, gave me the time I needed to get my head around what he was saying. He said he wanted to take an X-ray to be certain, but suggested I needed Tommy John surgery to repair the ligament in my elbow, and here my attitude softened, but only a little. My back was still up, however, because I stiff-armed the idea of surgery. In those days, the surgery meant at least a full year of rest and rehab, with no guarantees of a successful outcome—I wasn't liking the odds, or the ordeal that came with them. I weighed where I was in my career and what I'd accomplished, against where I was going and what there was still to accomplish, figured it had been a pretty good run: eight full seasons, a hundred-plus wins, a thousand-plus strikeouts, ten shutouts . . . a World Series ring! I imagined my stat line in the *Baseball Encyclopedia* and decided it was about what I deserved, about what I'd imagined.

I said, "Well, if I'm really at the end, Doc, I'm not going to have the surgery."

He was surprised, I think, by the certainty in my voice—said, "You'll be pitching with a compromised ligament. It could go at any time."

I said, "I'm already pitching with a compromised ligament." (Again with the attitude.)

I left Dr. Yocum's office that day just a little more informed than I'd been going in, and yet stitching a diagnosis to my struggles and knowing I had a career-threatening injury was an enormously liberating thing. In my head, that's how I chose to play it. No, it wasn't an approach that would work for everybody, but I told myself that I would go back out there and throw as hard as I could until my arm fell off. I would find a way to get people out . . . until I couldn't. Whatever it was that had me out of alignment, I would work my way through it. And do you know what? It freed me from worry, made me realize I'd been tentative on the mound, unwilling to push myself to any kind of limit.

The upshot: I was able to reinvent myself as a pitcher on the back of that visit to Dr. Yocum. I became more of an artist, and less of a thrower. I played with my delivery, adjusted my arm angle, added a bunch of new pitches to my arsenal—like a slow curveball I'd always been afraid to throw in a game situation. It was almost like free-form jazz, the way I started approaching each trip to the mound, each hitter, each situation. For years, I'd been throwing one way, playing music one way, and now with the knowledge that this ligament in my elbow could rupture with each toss, I was free to improvise . . . to find my way in an entirely new way.

I was making it up as I went along.

It was so cool. It reminded me of that great scene in the movie *The World According to Garp*, based on the John Irving novel, where Robin Williams is out with a Realtor looking at houses, and as he arrives at this one house he watches as a small plane crashes into the roof and then announces that he'll take it. The house is already disaster-proof, he says—and that's how Dr. Yocum's diagnosis left me feeling. Not like I was invincible, exactly, but like I knew what lay in wait, like there was nothing left for me to do but keep at it. Like nothing bad could happen—nothing worse, anyway, than I'd already imagined.

And so I kept at it.

And here's the thing: I turned my year around with this new mind-set. I did. I started pitching with abandon, strung together a bunch of strong starts, managed to go 14–8 the rest of the season, shaving almost two full runs off my ERA from the time of my visit with Dr. Yocum. Somewhere in there, I even put together that three-game sequence I wrote about earlier, against the Blue Jays, Yankees, and Blue Jays. Three complete games—two two-hit shutouts, bracketing a hard-luck 1–0 loss.

(For the record, one of those shutouts was the *synchronicity* game I pitched to Jamie Quirk.)

It would be the last great season of my career, and it was enough to earn me the last big contract of my career . . . *and* to help my Oakland teammates to the top spot in the American League West and my last appearance in the postseason.

(We lost to the Blue Jays in the AL Championship Series, which back then was just known as the playoffs.)

Let me tell you, it's a fine and fitting thing that this tour through my digest of former teammates lands on Dr. Yocum, for the way his diagnosis offered up a kind of grace note to my career, and gave me the permission I needed to pitch like an artist instead of *just* as an athlete. I wish I'd given myself the freedom to pitch in this way when I was twenty, when I was twenty-five, when there was the kind of life in my arm that would have stood as a formidable counterweight to this new sense of immediacy and creativity. I like to think I would have dominated, in ways I could never have imagined—but then, I came to pitching late, so I guess it would have taken me all this time anyway to mature in my approach. You need all those seasons to become well and truly seasoned, yes?

All along, my greatest assets as a pitcher had been my competitiveness and my athleticism—and the thing of it is, neither of those have a thing to do directly with pitching. The *art* of pitching . . . the *craft* of pitching . . . those elements came to me later, and in a lot of ways they came to me once I was able to shed this fear I didn't know I was carrying about throwing too much, too hard, too . . . *whatever.*

And so, I am ever grateful to Dr. Lewis Yocum, the noted orthopedic surgeon who helped me to salvage my career without lifting a scalpel—simply by gifting me the freedom to become the pitcher I was meant to be all along.

7

Head Games

The thing about baseball is that it catches the light of how we live and reflects it back to us in meaningful ways. We get out of it what we put into it, and even though on the surface it might seem like the game is about these groupings of singularly talented athletes coming together to outhustle, outwit, outperform these other groupings of singularly talented athletes, it's really about the human condition. It's about the flaws we discover in our character as we set about our days, how we get past them over the long slog of the season, how we don't . . . and, ultimately, how we adjust to the game's disappointments and try to set things right.

And—get this!—if we *don't* set things right and find a way to win, we content ourselves with the notion that there's always next year, so the game is also about renewal, redemption, rediscovery . . . good things all.

Forgive, please, these wistful musings on the meaning and measure of baseball, but as I look back on the characters I've met in a hundred baseball clubhouses I find myself thinking of the ways we prop up our hero athletes and ask them to stand as exemplars, role models. Alas, things are not always as they seem. One of the great gifts of my time as a broadcaster is the way it's opened me up to the narrative of the game, and I've come to realize that for every story of uplift and triumph there is one of struggle and loss. As a player, you tend to look at your teammates in simple terms: can he help you or hurt you? . . . lift you up or set you back? . . . amaze you or infuriate you? As a fan, it's much the same. You tend to forget that each and every player on the field has made it to the bigs after a young lifetime of being the very best at each stop along the way. They are who they have become because they have come to believe they can do no wrong. Or, at least, that's how it's always been . . . until the game changes things up on them, for it is in these upper reaches of the sport, playing alongside the best of the best, the toppermost of the poppermost, that ballplayers are no longer able to make things happen on the field simply by willing them so.

The other team is trying, too, remember? And it sometimes works out that *their* best is a little better than *your* best.

It's only after all these years in the broadcast booth, calling game after game, season after season, that I have come to appreciate the personalities on display, and the pressures ballplayers are under to play to the backs of their baseball cards and justify their big contracts. We might strut and bluster and move about the base paths like world-beaters, but there are weaknesses in the armor, all around. What's curious to me is that between the foul lines of a baseball diamond, where all these elite athletes meet to do their thing, you can still expect to find the same collection of quirky, nervous, compulsive behaviors you'll see in the rest of the wide, wide world, where everyday folks are made to shoulder the workaday stresses of everyday living. Professional baseball players are no different from anyone else. They fuss and fret and fight their own personal demons—with the one key difference being that they do these things on a very public stage.

I suppose I knew all of this as a player, but it's taken a second lifetime of *watching* the game for me to appreciate what's been right in front of me all along. Yep, there's a reason teams employ sports psychologists and motivational instructors to make sure their players' heads are screwed on straight. Indeed, behavior that might appear anywhere else as odd or slightly off can strike you as *very* odd and *way, way* off when it happens on a major league baseball field. I was reminded of this the very first time I took the mound in a big league game. I warmed up in the bullpen that day with Ron Hodges, who'd so humiliatingly welcomed me to the team with that disgusting wad of tobacco spittle just a few days earlier. The tradition, then as now, was for the backup catcher to get the starting pitcher warm. The starting catcher would then step in as you were finishing your warm-ups and take you the rest of the way. **Junior Ortiz** was the catcher on the day—a light-hitting backstop with a gun for an arm and a world-class glove. Junior had a season or two on me, but we were about the same age, and I was grateful to have him behind the plate for my major league debut instead of Hodges. The last thing I needed, with everything else swirling through my head as I made my first-ever start, was to have to work with a full-of-himself veteran who believed the rookies in his midst deserved to be treated like shit.

Plus, Junior was a *much* stronger defensive catcher . . . so there was *that*.

One thing about Junior, though—his English was lousy, and when he tried to power past the language barrier he fell into a serious stutter. I hate to even mention it, because it was just a simple speech impediment, brought about by nerves—and, perhaps, the feeling that because he couldn't speak the language he was somehow *less than*. And yet it was almost comical, the way Junior would wrestle with the words in his mouth. You could fry an egg in the time it took him to finish a sentence. I'd only been around the clubhouse for a couple days, but already I could see the other guys giving him a hard time about it—ballplayers not being the most sympathetic bunch, I guess. Let it be said, the razzing Junior received was far gentler than the razzing meted out by Ron Hodges and his ilk. It was more benign, more good-natured. The guys would bust Junior's balls, but only a little.

Anyway, I'd picked up on all of this, and found myself playing into it, so when Junior came out to the mound to get me settled before the start of the game, I waited for him to say what he'd come out to say. And then I waited some more. Poor Junior just couldn't get the words out. It's like his tongue had been taped to the roof of his mouth—that's how much difficulty he was having speaking.

Finally, I turned to him and said, "Junior, just fucking spit it out, will ya?"

He laughed—like a full-bodied, belly laugh—and after that the words started to flow. I'd let the air out of the situation and he was good to go. And it turned out that all he'd come to the mound to tell me was to relax and to wish me good luck, so it hardly seemed worth the trouble.

Wasn't like me, to make fun of someone for having a stutter, but this was baseball. This was where you learned there was no room for imperfection of any kind.

We were the best of the b-b-b-b-b-best, after all.

Years later, after I'd been traded to Oakland, I played alongside another athlete with a notable nervous tic—the right-handed pitcher **Steve Karsay**—only in this instance the twitch that had attached to him had somehow morphed into an asset. Steve was a hard-throwing rookie during my second full season with the A's—a kid from Queens who looked to all the world like he was headed for a huge career. In fact, he'd go on to grab a curious place in Mets history, when he gave up the historic post-9/11 home run to Mike Piazza that fairly ignited Shea Stadium and helped to lift the pall that had hung over New York City since the collapse of the Twin Towers.

Steve managed to put together a formidable career as journeyman pitcher, mostly in middle relief, going on to pitch for four additional teams before returning to the A's for one swan song season. But he earns a spot in these pages for a strange throwing motion he'd developed that really stood out. He had this unorthodox way of holding a runner on first—I'd never seen anything like it. He would look *behind* him, over his back shoulder. Picture it: as a right-hander, Steve's body would be facing third base when he went into his stretch. Every other right-handed pitcher in the game would look down his chin and peer over his left shoulder toward first base, to keep an eye on the runner. But Steve would come set and look back toward second base, over his *right* shoulder, sneaking a peak at the runner on first out of the corner of his right eye. It was the kind of subtle difference a typical fan might not notice at first, but we pitchers sure noticed. The coaching staff, too. They tried to get Steve to undo a lifetime habit, but he couldn't shed his routines. The motion was built into his hardwiring by this point, to where when he tried to hold the runner on in the conventional way, he couldn't jump-start his delivery and throw to the plate with his usual accuracy or velocity. And, if the runner on first was looking a little too *runner-ish,* Steve had a tough time going into his pickoff move.

It might have made all the sense in the world for him to look down and forward, but he was cut in this different way. He was stuck.

Nowadays, I see right-handed pitchers look over their back shoulder all the time when they're holding a runner on, because they've discovered it offers a wider field of vision. This is the asset that came about on the back of Steve's one little oddity, and I can certainly appreciate how holding a runner on in this way can open up the entire left side of the infield and allow you to check runners on second and third as well. But in Steve's day, which started at the end of *my* day there was no one else holding runners on in quite this way, so it was seen as a behavior in need of modification.

A final few words on that post-9/11 game: recall, the Braves had taken a one-run lead in the eighth, and Steve came on to start the bottom half of the inning. With one out, he walked Edgardo Alfonzo, and then he gave up the dinger to Mike Piazza—probably one of the most iconic home runs in team history. With that one swing, Mike helped to lift the spirit of the city, and to keep the Mets' slim playoff hopes alive in the last weeks of the season.

I remember feeling for Steve, because I knew full well what it was like to give up a meaningful, scene-shaping home run. But, knowing Steve and his Queens roots, I imagine it was an emotional moment for him as well, to see his city start to heal in this unexpected way, from a kind of front-row seat he hadn't really sought.

No, he wasn't rooting for Mike Piazza or the Mets in this spot, but I'm sure there was a part of him, deep down, that couldn't help but stand and cheer.

J unior Ortiz's stutter and Steve Karsay's back-shoulder pickoff look weren't the only tics or twitches or peculiarities I'd encounter during my time in the game, but they were two of the most memorable I got to see firsthand. Of course, I'd come of age as a ballplayer in the shadow of another pitcher from the Worcester, Massachusetts, area named **Mark Fidrych**, famously known as "The Bird" for his uncanny resemblance to *Sesame Street*'s Big Bird, but also for some of his goofy, quirky behavior on the mound. If you remember, Mark became a pop cultural phenomenon when he burst onto the scene with the Tigers in 1976, and captivated fans with the way he would talk to the ball and pat down the mound. He was like a folk hero in his rookie year, landing himself on the covers of *Sports Illustrated* and *Rolling Stone,* and on the mound to start the All-Star Game.

I was still in high school at the time, and a lot of the guys I was playing with and against had played with Mark, so his success and his strange behaviors were the talk of the region. Years later, I'd hear from Mark's critics, who claimed his many affectations on the mound were calculated to distract opposing hitters, but from the outside looking in they'd always struck me as a natural by-product of his goofy, quirky personality.

But there was never anything *wrong* with Mark Fidrych beyond his runaway exuberance. He was flaky, that's all, but in the buttoned-down, traditional world of baseball, that flakiness was sometimes seen as a tic or a peccadillo—something to be studied and analyzed instead of embraced and enjoyed.

There was another would-be superstar who briefly lit the baseball skies in and around Boston with his abundant talent and the promise of what lay ahead. **Rogelio Moret** was a lanky left-handed pitcher from Puerto Rico who could throw serious heat. Trouble was, the heat was a little all over the place. Later on in his career, Rogelio would go by the name of Roger—that's the name he put on his baseball card, and the one they used in the box scores when he finally made it to the bigs—but I first heard it as Rogelio, and that's the name that stayed with me. The Red Sox drafted him out of high school in 1968, around the time I was starting to follow the game in my own obsessive-compulsive ways, and once he was on my radar I tracked his every move on the field. The speed guns they used in those days weren't always the most reliable, but it was said that Rogelio could throw the ball 100 miles an hour. Today, there might be a couple pitchers on every big league staff capable of hitting triple digits, but back then . . . not so much.

Speed alone wasn't enough to earn Rogelio a steady gig. His control problems left him shuttling from Boston to Pawtucket to Louisville over parts of three seasons, and I would chart his comings and goings and root for the day when he would start striking out batters like nobody's business. He'd pitch with flashes of brilliance, and then he'd lose the plate. For a couple games, he'd be unhittable . . . and then, for a couple games, unwatchable.

He finally put it together toward the end of the 1974 season, when he almost no-hit the Chicago White Sox at Fenway—a complete game shutout, with 12 strikeouts. (The one hit he allowed that day was an infield single to Dick Allen—see how it all ties in!) Rogelio started the 1975 season in the bullpen, but pitched his way into the fifth spot of the rotation for the second half, posting a 14–3 record on the season and earning the praise of none other than Bill Lee, the "Spaceman" himself, with more than a few idiosyncrasies of his own, who credited Rogelio with putting the Red

Sox into contention, claiming that it was his emergence as a starter that allowed the team's established starters to pitch with a little extra rest (and a little extra bullpen certainty).

Rogelio's story took a dark turn a couple years later, after he'd been traded to the Texas Rangers and he fell into a kind of catatonic state one day at Arlington Stadium. His teammates later said he'd been behaving bizarrely, and then a group of them noticed Rogelio frozen in front of his locker for the longest time. At first, the other players thought he was fooling around, and they tried to joke him out of it, but eventually the team's medical staff was brought in and Rogelio was taken to a nearby psychiatric hospital. One of the Rangers players said it looked like they were removing a statue from the clubhouse—that's the condition Rogelio was in when they took him away.

He was released from the hospital a few days later, but Rogelio Moret never again pitched in the major leagues, and to this day nobody seems to know what might have triggered the episode. To those who knew him, who played with him, who followed the game, it went down as just one of those things—a sad, strange reminder that the weight of the game can sometimes be too much for a ballplayer to carry.

Perhaps the best illustration of the frailty of the American ballplayer is a condition that's come to be known as *the yips*. It's the term used to describe the sudden and often incomprehensible loss of fine motor skills in experienced, accomplished athletes, and it's not unique to baseball. Indeed, the term comes from the world of golf, where it is often attributed to the legendary champion Tommy Armour, winner of three majors, who found himself unable to sink his short putts during the Shawnee Open, just one week after winning the 1927 U.S. Open. Armour ended up carding the first-ever *Archaeopteryx*—18 over par for a 23 on this one par 5 hole, to this date the highest-score ever on a single hole in PGA history.

(Thanks, Wikipedia!)

In baseball, the first time I ever heard of a ballplayer who suddenly and inexplicably lost his ability to throw accurately was when the Pirates' **Steve Blass** unraveled in the 1973 season. He'd been a World Series champion in 1971, and an All-Star in 1972, and in 1973 he could only pitch to a 9.85 ERA, averaging about a walk per inning. It was such a remarkable transformation that sportswriters diagnosed his condition as "Steve Blass disease," and for years the term stuck to him like shit on your shoe.

In fact, the term stuck until one of my first broadcast partners came along about ten years later. **Steve Sax** was a perennial All-Star second baseman for the Los Angeles Dodgers—one of the game's great table-setters. As a pitcher, I never liked facing those Dodger teams of the mid-1980s. They could hurt you in so many ways, and Steve was at the heart of a great many of those ways. But early on in his career, right after his All-Star, Rookie of the Year debut in 1982, he couldn't make the simple throw to first from the second base slot. His mechanics were all screwy, and he labored mightily to keep his job—*and* to keep his team in the game. Just to make things worse, sportswriters weighed in and started referring to his condition as "Steve Sax Syndrome"—a dubious honor for a twenty-three-year-old kid to carry.

Steve managed to keep his spot in the lineup for most of that year. The Dodgers were patient with him as he tried to work his way through his troubles. Still, he ended up making 30 errors that year, most of them throwing errors, but that number doesn't even get close to the number of times he held the ball a couple beats too long and cost his team a shot at a double play, or the number of times he might have lollipopped or underhanded the ball to first because he couldn't get off a decent throw.

One of the all-time great lines to emerge from Steve's "lost" season of 1983 came from his Dodger teammate Pedro Guerrero, the Dominican slugger. Pedro was an outfielder by trade, but he was asked to play third base for a stretch of games that year. When a reporter asked him what he was thinking about as he went into his crouch before each pitch, Pedro allowed that his first thought was, *I hope they don't hit it to me.* His second thought? *I hope they don't hit it to Sax.*

I ended up working with Steve on my very first broadcasting gig—an afternoon show for Fox Sports called *Baseball Today.* Steve was the main host, and I traded sidekick duties with former Royals pitcher Mark Gubicza. The show was set up that way because the producer, Hank Siegel, wasn't sure Mark and I were up to the job. I'd work one week in Los Angeles with Steve, and then Mark would step in for his week with Steve, and we went back and forth like that for the next while.

From time to time, Steve and I would get to talking, but we never really talked about his struggles in the field. Ballplayers didn't like to talk about this type of thing. Anything that made them come across as weak or *less than* or vulnerable . . . that was off the table. It's like we have to put out this macho front, when in reality everyone who's ever played the game has had a moment or two when it feels to him like the game has gotten away from him. But Steve and I didn't have to talk about the yips for me to know his mind, and the more I got to know him, the more I came to appreciate his confidence. He was completely relaxed on-set, and around even the most intimidating television executives, and I mention this here for the way it stands in such sharp contrast to the tentative ways he played when he was having all that trouble throwing the ball. The one didn't seem to jibe with the other . . . and yet there it was.

As I've written, Steve Sax was a bit of a nemesis in my career, a guy I never wanted to face, but there was one time in particular when he cost me a moment—indeed, it might have been one of the very finest moments of my career, were it not for Saxy. He was in the on-deck circle, bases loaded, one out, when the Dodgers put on the squeeze. It just worked out that I had it read the whole way. I came running in from the mound, and scooped up the bunt with a pretty little shovel-and-dive move that just nipped the runner at the plate—one of the greatest defensive plays I'd ever made, at any level. As a pitcher, I always prided myself on my contributions with my glove or my bat, and this one was right up there. But then Saxy strode to the plate and promptly stroked a single up the middle, scoring the runners from second and third. Just like that, my pretty defensive gem was erased, irrelevant, beside the point. If I'd some-how gotten out of that inning, it would have been a personal highlight, and now it was as if it never even happened.

On the highlight reel of my career that occasionally plays in my head, this defensive "gem" that was and wasn't stands as the home version of **Endy Chavez**'s near-legendary grab from Game 7 of the 2006 National League Championship Series against the Cardi-nals, when he plucked a two-run home run off the bat of Scott Rolen from the left field bullpen. Recall, the score was tied 1–1 in the sixth inning, one out, runner on first, when Endy fairly soared over the fence to make the grab and then fired to first to double-up the runner to end the inning. It was an eye-popping play, an all-time stunner, and it would have been remembered by Mets fans with great reverence instead of mere fondness if Yadier Molina didn't step to the plate in the ninth inning and stroke a two-run homer of his own, this one well beyond Endy's superhuman reach, to end the Mets' season.

In my head at least, this shovel-and-dive play against Steve Sax's Dodgers was like that . . . a little.

Happily, Steve's yips were short-lived—or, at least, he found a way to power past them and let muscle memory take over. He went on to make a couple more All-Star teams, and to make his mark on the game for another ten years. We even crossed paths as teammates for a short while in Oakland—Steve's last stop in his fourteen-year career.

Somewhat less happily, the *other* similarly afflicted Steve, Steve Blass, was never given the chance to right himself—perhaps because his condition found him late in his career. The silver lining here, though, was that Steve was such a beloved figure to Pirates fans that he was able to segue into the team's broadcast booth, where he worked as a color commentator for over twenty years, and I offer their stories here with admiration and sympathy for what these two competitors endured . . . feelings I wish I could attach to the story I'm about to share about a former battery-mate who famously fought his own battle with the yips.

Mackey Sasser.
The name alone can excite/enrage/entertain Mets fans of a certain age, depending on his/her point of view.

My point of view came from a place of frustration, because from where I stood on the mound I could only look on and wonder—and curse the baseball gods for putting me in a spot where my catcher couldn't even get the ball back to me without making me sweat.

Perhaps a little setup is in order . . .

Mackey joined the Mets ahead of the 1988 season, in a trade with the Pirates, ostensibly to back up Gary Carter behind the plate. Mackey was known in those days for his bat and his arm. Really, he was a helluva hitter, which during my time in the game was a bit of a luxury—to have *two* catchers on your roster who could hit a ton should have given us an edge, going into the season. And it did, for a while . . . until a collision at home plate left Mackey with one of the worst cases of the yips I'd ever seen or heard about or been forced to play through.

Out of nowhere, Mackey started double-clutching on his routine throws back to the mound. Or he'd have to tap his glove two, three, or four times before releasing the ball. It was almost painful to watch him agonize over getting the ball back to the pitcher, especially when you stopped to realize that when the ball was in play he could barehand a slow roller up the first base line and fire to first for the out, or gun down a runner trying to steal second. It's when he had all the time in the world between pitches that he found a way to fill it with a whole lot of weirdness.

Now, I don't mean to dismiss Mackey's difficulties, or to trivialize them in any way. The yips are a very real, diagnosable condition, covering a constellation of twitches and glitches in any number of practiced behaviors relating to a very specific fine motor skill—say, throwing a baseball, or sinking a putt, or playing darts. Basically, anything involving a repetitive motion that's been developed over time and grooved into routine. As an organization, the Mets went out of their way to help Mackey through this. They set him up with a sports psychiatrist, a physical therapist . . . they tried everything.

But what they *didn't* do was talk to the team. The rest of us were *yips adjacent,* and I'm sure it would have helped Mackey to know that his teammates were on his side—which, sad to say, we weren't.

There's been a lot of research into what might cause the yips, and nobody's come up with a surefire way to cure them. Sometimes, they go away on their own—leaving the poor sod who endured them to forever wonder if and when they'll return. And sometimes, they don't—putting an effective end to an athletic career. They seem to surface in a problematic way with top-level athletes who have spent a lifetime perfecting certain specific aspects of their sport, and I think it gnaws at those of us who played the game to think how easily it could have been *us* on the jittery end of these worries.

In baseball, every pitcher who's being completely honest with himself (and with his coaches!) goes through a stage when he stands on the mound and has no idea where the ball is going. Maybe the baseball just doesn't feel right in his hands, or a certain arm angle is no longer comfortable. Most times, the feeling lasts for just a couple pitches or so, and if you're lucky those pitches happen during your warm-up. We've all seen it: a reliever comes on to put out a rally and sails his first pitch all the way to the backstop. Usually, it's just nerves, and once you settle in to the game or the situation the ball once again feels right and true.

It's when the feeling becomes chronic that it can derail a career, like it very nearly did with Steve Sax, and like it almost certainly did with Steve Blass. With Mackey Sasser, it threatened to derail our entire season, because as a catcher he had to handle the ball after every single pitch. His presence in the lineup changed the mood of the entire clubhouse . . . and not to the good. Nobody on the staff wanted to pitch to him, because he could barely get the ball back to the mound. Sometimes, he'd roll it, like a bowling ball.

Or he'd loft an underhanded toss that would fall like a teardrop into the no-man's-land in front of second base. Teams around the league were of course well aware of Mackey's shortcomings in this area, and they used their scouting reports to full advantage. Base runners on first would anticipate one of his lollipop throws and scamper to second in the time it took the ball to find its way back to the pitcher—a move that would go down as a stolen base, even though it always felt to me like it was closer to catcher's indifference . . . or, cruelly, catcher's incompetence.

I must've pitched to Mackey thirty, forty times during our overlapping tenures in New York, and each time out it was an adventure wrapped inside an enigma. I can remember standing on the mound for what always felt to me like an interminable period of time, wondering if and how and when he'd get the ball back to me. Often, I'd have to finish my delivery and start walking toward the plate, meeting Mackey halfway so he could hand the ball back to me. Sometimes, he'd drop it in my glove and then pat me on the butt to make it seem like we were meeting to discuss how to pitch to the next batter, or some other piece of strategy—a charade that always pissed me off for the way it suggested that Mackey was somehow running the show from behind the plate.

(You know, as I set these words to paper I can't help but wonder how these meet-in-the-middle hand-offs would be treated alongside the rules changes in today's game, when trips to the mound are now limited.)

Occasionally, if there were runners on when Mackey was catching, I'd have to drop to my knees to "block" one of his errant throws and try to keep the ball in front of me, and whenever that happened I'd think, *What the fuck? He's supposed to be the one blocking my throws.*

No question, we were vulnerable with Mackey behind the plate, but Davey Johnson kept trotting him out because Mackey could hit. Oh, man . . . Mackey could hit. His bat kept him in the game—and, got to admit, there were times I caught myself wishing he'd fall into the kind of prolonged slump at the plate that would leave management to reevaluate his abilities versus his liabilities.

He wasn't my favorite teammate, let's just say that. And it wasn't because of the yips. I mean, the yips were a part of it, to be sure, but you'd think, when a guy's struggling like that . . . when he's become a burden to his teammates . . . when he *knows* he's become a burden to his teammates . . . when everyone around him is extending a kind of helping hand, he might go out of his way to apologize for putting us all in a tough spot. Or, at least, to acknowledge what was going on. But Mackey wasn't like that. He just went about his business and seemed to assume that all these little brushfires he was setting off around him when he took the field were someone else's problem.

Remember those old Mr. Magoo cartoons, where Magoo would "blindly" cross the street and there'd be these ten-car pile-ups all around him while he continued to move about oblivious to the commotion he was causing? Well, Mackey Sasser was like that. We were all jumping through hoops to accommodate his condition, and he didn't even seem to notice.

On top of all that, he wasn't the most responsible teammate in the world. He was the kind of guy who wouldn't get his rest before a game. He could be out until five o'clock in the morning when we had a day game the next afternoon—not exactly the best way to endear yourself to your teammates who were already scrambling to clean up your messes on the field.

No, it wasn't Mackey's fault that he came down with the yips. It's a terrible hardship I wouldn't wish on anyone. And no, same way it wasn't like me to make fun of someone like Junior Ortiz for a simple stutter, it wasn't like me to begrudge someone a nervous tic he couldn't control. And yet I came away from this episode thinking Mackey had somehow made a mockery of the game. To have a guy behind the plate who couldn't even get the ball back to his pitcher . . . that's not the way the game should be played. The optics are all wrong. The message we're putting out to our young fans, who come to the ballpark looking for players to root for, to put on some kind of pedestal, is completely off. I suppose on some level it could have been seen as inspiring, for a guy like Mackey to power through this kind of turmoil and still find a way to contribute, but his limitations invariably seemed to cancel out his contributions. His performances needed to be judged with the baseball equivalent of the plus-minus stat they keep in hockey: you drive in two runs, you let in two runs, and you're treading water.

For all these reasons, and a few more that I won't share because I don't want to come across as completely unsympathetic, I was always looking for ways to get back at Mackey for diminishing the game in this way. One night in Atlanta, I found a way to give him his comeuppance. A group of us were out at a club, and Mackey was making eyes at this beautiful Asian girl across the way. He kept going on and on about how gorgeous she was, asking some of us if we thought he stood a chance with her. This went on for a while, until I excused myself to go to the bathroom, and who should sidle up to the urinal next to mine but this beautiful Asian girl— who, alas, was a dude.

In all fairness to Mackey, this guy was probably the best-looking guy I'd ever seen. His makeup and hair were killer, and his little cocktail dress looked like it had been painted on. But all of that seemed to fall away when he lifted his skirt and whipped himself out and started taking a piss.

He caught me staring—said, "You okay?"

I said, "Oh, I'm fine. But my friend's in for a surprise."

The guy laughed and said, "Don't I know it."

I went back out to join our group and started chatting up Mackey, told him I'd just run into that beautiful Asian girl on my way to the bathroom. I said, "She's even prettier up close."

That was all he needed to hear. And then, when my bathroom buddy sauntered over to our table, I stood and made an introduction.

They ended up leaving together, and for all I know they went back to Mackey's room, but I never asked, and I never said anything. It would have been too easy to bust his chops about it the next day, but I chose to walk the high road on this—or, at least, the road a notch or two above the gutter. I didn't want to give him the satisfaction of knowing that I'd set him up in this way, or that it was even worth it to me to mess with him.

It was enough for me to know . . . and, now, for *everyone* to know.

I can't write an entire chapter about the yips without spending some time on one of the most surprising, most inspiring stories I've had a chance to witness as a broadcaster . . . and as a fan. The story actually found me at first in my living room, watching Game 1 of the 2000 National League Division Series between the Atlanta Braves and the St. Louis Cardinals. The Cardinals' brilliant rookie pitcher **Rick Ankiel** was on the mound, facing Greg Maddux—a marquee matchup that had baseball's attention.

Of course, I tuned in. And like millions of caring, feeling fans, I cringed when I saw Ankiel begin to struggle with his control in the third inning. Actually, to merely suggest that this young man was struggling doesn't get close to the size of his troubles on that mound. It was a complete breakdown: four runs on two hits, four walks, and five wild pitches, before being pulled from the game with two outs in the inning.

I watched what was happening with a heavy heart. I knew what it was to have one of *those* moments. Every pitcher has experienced it—at one time or another, in one fashion or another. Usually, it's just a fleeing moment, there for a couple seconds, maybe a couple pitches. Maybe it lasts a little bit longer, but we've all been there. We've all had that terrifying sensation where the ball feels foreign and you think, *Whoa!* Or, *Holy shit!*

Somehow, the Cardinals managed to hold on to win the game, and Rick Ankiel was able to joke about his blip of a performance in the press conference afterward, talking about how it felt to tie a record that had stood for over a hundred years and had been thought unassailable—throwing five wild pitches in a single inning. For the time being at least, those of us who cared about such things could tell ourselves Ankiel's third-inning performance was an aberration and that he would return to form the next time he took the hill.

Surely, Ankiel was telling himself the same thing.

But that's not exactly what happened. Ankiel's next start came the following week in Game 2 of the National League Championship Series against the Mets, and this time he didn't even get out of the first inning. His very first pitch of the game went straight over the head of Mets leadoff hitter Timo Perez, and right away it was clear that Ankiel was still stuck, and that the pitcher he was wouldn't be returning to the mound anytime soon.

My old skipper Tony La Russa, now managing the Cardinals, trotted Ankiel out again in Game 5 of the series, this time in a relief role, and here again the kid couldn't throw strikes. The ball must have felt so completely unfamiliar in his grip, and I ached for him, to see him so hopelessly lost at such a young age, on such a grand stage. I mean, it's not like he was pitching on some random Tuesday night in Pittsburgh in a meaningless game. No, this was the postseason. This was everything. The eyes of the baseball world were upon him. That's quite a lot of pressure to put on a set of young shoulders.

Just to be clear, nobody knows if it was the weight of all that pressure that got to Rick Ankiel during those postseason games. No one can say if the youngster was battling the kind of personal demons that got in the way of his game plan, and messed with the mechanics he'd developed over a lifetime.

All we know is what we saw, and what we saw were the yips . . . on full display. From out of nowhere.

Years later, in Buzz Bissinger's excellent book *Three Nights in August,* chronicling a three-game series between the Cubs and the Cardinals, La Russa allowed that starting Ankiel in Game 1 of the Atlanta series was one of the deepest regrets of his career, for the way it put him in a spot that was perhaps too big for his résumé. La Russa blamed himself for Ankiel's meltdown.

Ankiel, to his great credit, wasn't buying it. This was on him, he always said, not La Russa.

Ankiel would go on to write his own book about his experiences—*The Phenomenon: Pressure, the Yips, and the Pitch That Changed My Life,* written with the baseball journalist Tim Brown. It's one of the best books I've ever read—about baseball, about life, about *anything.* In it, Ankiel confronts those dark days when he lost the ability to pitch, and that agonizing off-season after those dreadful October games, when he was left to wonder if he would ever pitch again.

He did, but not effectively. He suffered through another few miserable outings to start the 2001 season, before the Cardinals put him on the disabled list to try to get his head right. After that, he was out of baseball for a couple years, before fighting his way back to the big club for a handful of nothing-special appearances as a September call-up.

And that was that . . . except it *wasn't*. You see, Rick Ankiel happened to be a tremendous athlete, and an outstanding hitter. As good a hitter as I *thought* I was, he was ten times better. Plus, he had a fire inside him like you wouldn't believe. He got it in his head that he would reinvent himself as a ballplayer, and find a way to make it back to the bigs as a position player—something no one in the game could remember having seen since the transformation of Babe Ruth from one of baseball's preeminent pitchers into the stuff of legend.

(Of course, this was long before anyone in the United States had ever *heard* of Shohei Ohtani, the Angels' sensational two-way player, but that's a whole other story.)

Jump ahead to August 2007, and Ankiel's transformation was complete. A supportive Cardinals organization gave him every opportunity to succeed as a position player, and Ankiel earned himself a roster spot. He homered in his very first game—a three-run blast to right in the bottom of the seventh against the San Diego Padres.

It was the shot heard 'round the world, revisited. Ankiel's redemption—if, indeed, that's what it was—was played and replayed on ESPN's *SportsCenter,* and on other sports highlight shows across the country, until he came back two games later and hit another couple dingers. He finished the season batting .285, with 11 home runs and 39 RBIs in just 47 games.

Not bad for a pitcher.

Not bad for a twenty-eight-year-old rookie slugger.

Not bad at all.

What I loved about Rick Ankiel's story was the courageous way he would not let himself be defined by a series of low, low moments when the game ran away from him. It was a remarkable thing to see—amazing, really. I suppose, if Ankiel's comeback had been a bust and he never made it as a bona fide position player, the albatross of those 2000 postseason games would have stamped him a failure, a victim of the yips, his promising career cut short before it every really got under way.

He was not about to let that happen.

I had a chance to see this young man's renaissance firsthand the following season, when the Mets finally drew the Cardinals on the calendar during the first week in July. By this point, Ankiel had chased the skeptics who might have thought he was some sort of flash in the pan and locked down a spot as the team's everyday center fielder. That he could play the field well enough to man one of the most demanding positions on the diamond was . . . *something*.

That he could also hit the hell out of the ball was something else again.

I was anxious to see this kid play, and he didn't disappoint. He homered in the first two games of the series, and I stood and cheered. It was a good and thrilling thing to see, because in these moments of Ankiel's resurrection and triumph there was the wistful, chilling thought that the wildness or the nerves or the *whatever* that had nearly cost this kid his career could have very easily happened to me . . . to any of the hundreds of pitchers I'd played with and against in my career. It was one of those *there but for the grace of God go I* moments, and I reveled in the fact that this courageous and gifted young man had somehow clawed his way back from ignominy with his iron will, his mighty bat, his supreme athleticism.

I found some time to talk to Ankiel before the Mets left town. I skulked around the Cardinal clubhouse the next day, and roamed the field during batting practice, looking for a moment where I might catch him alone. I didn't want to embarrass him in front of his teammates or anything. I just wanted to shake his hand, maybe congratulate him on his turnaround.

When I finally caught up to him, I made like a broadcaster and engaged him with the usual small talk. It was just a quick conversation. But then, as we made to part, I turned back to him and said, "Hey, man. Just want to let you know, we're all proud of you."

And we were. The collective baseball *we*. The game itself.

8

"Z" Is for "Zimmer"

To be clear, we're done with the alphabetically themed portions of the book, but I had it in my head that there'd be an "Aase to Zimmer" element on the contents page, so I'm sticking with the "A is for . . ." construct for the title to this chapter—a look back at some of the managers I've encountered on my baseball journey. Some of them, I've played for. Some of them, I've played against. Some, I've merely encountered . . . but I'll shine a light on them here for the various ways they've enlightened me, infuriated me, or amused the hell out of me.

Let's start it off with **Don Zimmer**, who already made a cameo early on in these pages, just as he did early on in my career. Recall, he was the Texas Rangers manager when I went to my very first big league spring training camp, and almost from the very moment he watched me pitch he let me know that I had graduated to a whole other level of the game. The first time I appeared in a spring training game for the Rangers was against the New York Yankees, in Fort Lauderdale, in front of a packed house. In those days, you didn't always see big crowds at our Grapefruit League games, but the Yankees were always a big draw.

You might think an exhibition game, with nothing on the line beyond getting your feet wet against big league ballplayers, is a no-pressure situation. But I was feeling jittery, tense, and looking back I think the big crowd played into that. Still, I managed to pitch three or four clean innings. I no longer remember how many hits I gave up, how many base runners I allowed, and there's no surviving box score, but I was generally happy with my performance: nobody scored, and I'd retired a bunch of big league hitters, so I counted it a successful outing.

I sat down on the dugout bench after what would turn out to be my last inning and Don Zimmer walked over to me—said, "That's it for you today, kid. I got someone else coming in."

I nodded—said, "Okay, Skip."

(By the way, this was the first time I'd addressed Zimmer, other than to nod hello or to smile stupidly, and I'd been going back and forth in my head over whether to call him Skip or Mr. Zimmer or maybe even Sir. Now that I had a couple clean innings under my belt, I guess I decided to lean toward the familiar.)

With this, Zimmer turned to go, but then he doubled back—said, "Stick around for a sec. Something I want to talk to you about."

I nodded again—only this time I was thinking, *What did I do?* I thought maybe I'd screwed up in some way, and that I was about to be called to the woodshed for my first big league dressing-down.

When our guys took the field for the next inning, Zimmer came over to me again and sat himself down. He asked to see my glove. I thought that was strange, but I handed it to him—because, hey, when you're at your first big league camp and your manager asks to see your glove, you show him your glove. He looked it over and set it down. Then he turned to me and said, "You were an infielder in college, right?"

I said, "Yes, sir."

He said, "You were pretty good, right?"

I said, "Oh, I don't know about that."

He said, "And you could hit some, too, from what I hear?"

I had no idea where Zimmer was going with this, was starting to feel a little embarrassed, so I tried to turn the conversation away from my hitting and my fielding—said, "That didn't exactly work out for me."

He handed my glove back to me—said, "That's what I wanted to talk to you about." Then he pointed back to my glove and said, "This glove right here. You gotta get rid of it."

Hadn't seen that one coming. I loved that glove. I'd had it in college. It was like an old friend. But Don Zimmer slipped his left hand into it and flipped it over, palm down. It had an open back, of course, like most infielders' gloves. I was in the habit of resting my index finger on the leather outside the finger slot, like most infielders. Today's infielders have a protective leather covering that rests atop the glove leather, to shield that stray finger, but back then we had no such luxury.

With his right hand, Zimmer pointed to the exposed part of his left hand in the glove and said, "Get yourself a closed glove, son. No opening in the back."

I nodded—wasn't about to go against my manager, even though I had no idea what he was talking about. But then he explained himself and it all came clear. He said, "See this open back? Every time you throw a curveball, you move your finger. You're letting the hitter know."

That's the astonishing thing about a baseball lifer like Don Zimmer. He could spot a tell from a mile away. He'd watched me pitch for just three innings, from about a hundred feet away, and he very quickly picked up that I was giving away my curveball.

Welcome to the big leagues, huh?

The first manager I actually *played* for as a professional was **Tom Burgess**—a Canadian-born first baseman who (weirdly) had a couple cups of coffee in the bigs. The first was a brief stint with the Cardinals in 1954, when he was twenty-six years old. The second was a full season with the Angels eight years later, in 1962, when he was thirty-four. You had to admire this guy's perseverance, right? And yet it wasn't until Tom Burgess started managing in the low-level minors that he found his true calling in the game—and he stuck around a good long while after that, eventually coaching third base for the New York Mets, under manager Joe Torre, and for the Atlanta Braves, under Bobby Cox.

Tom was managing the Double-A Tulsa Drillers of the Texas League, where I was sent following the 1981 amateur draft—just a couple months after I'd thrown my last pitch for the Yale Bulldogs. I joined the team in Shreveport, where the upper deck of the stadium was roped off because it had been condemned by the local building department. That was my "Welcome to Professional Baseball" moment. Didn't exactly feel like the big time, I'll say that. There was a guy outside the stadium selling weed, and a straight-up Baseball Annie brazenly pimping out her daughter outside the players' entrance . . . all told, nothing to indicate that I had arrived.

After having been somewhat coddled as a ballplayer in my time at Yale, I could see that my tour of duty in the Texas League would be a comedown wrapped inside a letdown and served with a side helping of an emotional beatdown. Forget the ramshackle surroundings and the general shit show that greeted us as we played out our schedule—it was the miserable way I was treated by my Tulsa teammates that would stamp my first professional season. Nobody said as much, but I could see straightaway that I was in for a bit of a hazing—with an extra layer or two of benign cruelty kicked my way in consideration of the fact that I was the Rangers' first-round draft choice. Apparently, my first-round status entitled me to change into my uniform while seated on the cement floor in the middle of that Shreveport locker room, and to lay out my things beneath a ratty picnic table.

(The actual lockers were reserved for the veteran players and our later-round draft picks who somehow hadn't landed on the same shit list next to my name.)

My lowly status as a top draft pick also meant I didn't rate a berth on the sleeper bus we rode, for the long hauls to Little Rock and Amarillo and Jackson, Mississippi.

It would have been nice if there was some sort of guardian angel on hand to give me the lay of this particular land, but I was left to figure it all out for myself. Tom Burgess helped—not a lot, but some. He was substantially older than his players—in his mid-fifties—so he operated at some remove from the usual shenanigans and rituals. No, he wasn't about to assign me a locker, or help me find a place to sleep on one of our twenty-hour bus rides . . . that would have gone against baseball code. But he was quick to smile, and to pat me on the back, and to offer up some heartfelt words of encouragement like, "Hang in there, kid."

He was also quick to pull out a deck of cards, which was the way he and some of the coaches passed the time on the bus or in the locker room—the age-appropriate (and era-appropriate!) version of the video games ballplayers distract themselves with today. Tom taught me how to play both Hearts and Spades, and I was an eager pupil. I'd grown up in a card-playing household, but for some reason we'd never played Hearts or Spades in my family—Pitch was our game, growing up—so this was new ground for me. I picked them both up pretty quick, and I got pretty good at them, too—good enough to make those overnight rides pass a little more quickly, because my asshole teammates *still* weren't letting me sleep on the bus.

Let me tell you, there's nothing quite so thrilling as the sight of a sunrise over Midland, Texas, as you pull into town knowing you'll have a couple hours to stretch out on the cement floor of *that* stadium and maybe catch a couple winks before game time.

In the Texas organization, our Double-A outpost in Tulsa was a kind of breeding ground for Ranger prospects. We had a lot of good young players on that team who'd go on to have decent major league careers: Pete O'Brien, who played first base for the Rangers for a stretch; George Wright, soon to be the team's center fielder; and Tom Henke, who became one of the game's top closers during his time with Toronto.

Looking back, I think the guys were a little rougher on me than they might have been in any other year, because when I joined the Drillers for the second half of the season, our big league counterparts were out on strike. Since there was no baseball at the major league level, the Rangers' beat writers didn't have a whole lot to write about, so I received an inordinate amount of coverage as the team's #1 pick.

I didn't ask for the attention, didn't particularly want it, but there it was—unnecessary roughness, of a kind—and every time a story appeared in one of the papers the older players took it as a signal to ratchet up the benign cruelty, which basically meant I could never count on sleeping anytime soon. Or changing in front of an actual locker. Or being served anything better than scraps whenever we sat (or, in my case, stood) for a team meal.

I remember being on the receiving end of all manner of pitying looks that summer from Tom Burgess, who seemed to really want to help me navigate the situation, but he was powerless to do so without upending the forces of good and evil that govern the geopolitical system of professional baseball. He could only flash a smile of encouragement, shuffle the deck of cards he seemed to always have at the ready, and deal me in.

It felt to me at times like I was in some Darwinian struggle, where I had only to survive these minor nuisances if I meant to make it to the next rung on the baseball ladder.

I just needed to figure it out, ride it out, in what ways I could.

My first year in the Mets organization was a complete waste of time. I don't think I realized it in the moment, but I was a bit of a mess, my head probably someplace else—Texas, most likely. You have to realize, I was brand spanking new to the business of professional baseball. I'd barely had time to wrap my head around the idea that I'd be playing for the Rangers, and now I had to process that I'd been traded from the organization that had drafted me, so it was a bit of an adjustment.

I was assigned to the Mets' Triple-A team in Tidewater, which as I wrote earlier was managed that year by *Jack Aker*, a former big league pitcher who'd had some good years with the A's and Yankees. Actually, *managed* is not exactly the right word in this context—it was more like Jack Aker *presided* over the team that year. He didn't do a whole lot of managing that I could see. He was just kind of there.

Frankly, I don't think Jack was too happy to have me in his

rotation, because my arrival pushed one of the arms he'd been counting on to the Mets' Double-A franchise, but Aker never said as much. As I also wrote earlier, he never said much of anything. For the entire season. He was the only person in baseball who was horrible to me—like, *actively* horrible. Here again, that might not be the best word. Perhaps it would be more accurate to say he was *passively* horrible, because all he did was give me the cold shoulder. He essentially ignored me the whole time I played for him. Really, I cannot recall one conversation I had with this man . . . not one. And the curious thing was he was recently divorced and had a girlfriend back then who was around a lot of the time, and *she* couldn't have been nicer to me. We used to have these great conversations, and as we talked I'd wonder what this great woman was doing with this asshole of a manager.

I've already shared a story or two about Frank Howard, my first big league manager when I was called up in 1983, but I've yet to mention **George Bamberger**, the Mets skipper at the start of the season. The team got off to a dreadful start that year—16–30, when Bamberger announced his resignation.

I never played for Bambi, but he had two of the all-time great lines when reporters chased him down for note and comment on his Mets tenure.

When asked why he was stepping away from the Mets job, he said, "I think I've suffered enough."

And when asked what he was going to do next, he said, "I'm going fishin'."

I remember thinking, *That about covers it.*

I had almost no relationship with Montreal manager **Tom Runnells**. For years and years I hadn't even thought about him, or my time in an Expos uniform in 1991 until I sat down to write this book, and even then he didn't come immediately to mind. The first time I scratched my head to see if I could come up with an anecdote to attach to my Expos career or my relationship with my manager there, I actually wrote down Buck Rodgers's name in this little notebook I kept with stories for this book. That's how little I remember from my time in Montreal.

Now, in fairness to me, Tom had replaced Buck as the Expos manager about a month before I arrived in Montreal, and I'd been led to believe that the trade to Montreal was a kind of stopgap maneuver after a planned three-way trade with the Mets-Expos-A's had failed to materialize, so I guess I put the whole experience out of my mind. Truth be told, it was never really *in there* in any kind of consequential way. For the two weeks I played for the Expos, my head was someplace else. At the time, I could never get a clear answer on what was going down, and what kind of snag may or may not have been hit in these talks that left me dangling in the Great White North, but I kept hearing whispered comments like, "I wouldn't unpack if I were you" and "Don't bother learning French"—which, taken together, left me thinking some other cleat was about to be dropped on my career.

Nothing against the great city of Montreal, or the Expos fans, but it felt to me like I was in limbo there. Too, it felt like I was unwanted. No one in the Expos organization knew quite what to do with me, what to make of me—and, in turn, I had no idea what to do with myself, or how I fit.

If I even fit at all.

I should mention here that one of the universal truths of the game is that when a player is released or traded, there's a tendency to block the moment from memory. It's like you're hit by Will Smith or Tommy Lee Jones with one of those neuralyzer devices from

Men in Black, and you can't remember shit. I happen to remember in great detail the moment I was released from the A's and was pushed to call it a career, because it happened to be my birthday and there were so many other moving parts to consider, but here when Frank Cashen called me in to tell me the Mets were trading me to Montreal, it's all a blur. I can remember six of my Mets teammates walking with me to Frank's office in a show of support, each of us knowing I was like a dead man walking, but after that I've got nothing. I couldn't tell you what Frank said, if there was anyone else from the Mets front office in the room with us . . . nothing. When I walked out, I was so dazed I don't think I could have even told you which team I'd been traded to.

Understand, I was a seasoned, hardened professional athlete by this point. It was nearly ten years since the last time I'd been traded, and I'd seen dozens of players come and go in all that time since. I knew this was how the game was played off the field. And, somehow, I knew enough to get myself to Montreal, where I was scheduled to make my next start on my usual rest.

And yet, that was all I knew, just then. And it's *still* all I know, except that the one start I thought I'd make for the Expos turned into another. And then another. The first start was in Montreal, and the next two were on the road. I pitched miserably—to a 7.41 ERA—and it was made clear to me that I wasn't in the team's plans.

Mercifully, I never made it back to Montreal after the one road trip I went on with the Expos. I was traded to the A's while we were in San Francisco, for two minor league pitchers, so I made the short trek across the bay to join my new team, where I told myself I belonged—and where, in fact, I would go on to post some of the best years of my career.

One footnote to my time in Montreal: I have only one specific memory of any of my Expos teammates, or any of the interactions we shared during my two weeks with the club. **Ron Hassey** was a veteran catcher, finishing out the string on his own career when I breezed through town, and he sought me out almost as soon as I arrived in the clubhouse. He wasn't looking to talk baseball, or to welcome me to the team, however. No, he just wanted to know if I played golf—not because he wanted to invite me to play a round with him at the next opportunity, but because he had a little sideline business going, selling golf balls.

Yep . . . that about summed up my Canadian sojourn, and thanks to Ron Hassey I came away from those two "lost" weeks thinking I was more valuable to my teammates as a potential customer than I was as a potential teammate.

One of the things the Mets are lousy at is honoring the team's past. All across baseball, organizations trot out their stars for Old Timers' Day ceremonies or throwback events to commemorate a meaningful franchise milestone, but I've come to the sad realization that the team's current owners might just believe the Mets' history began when they bought out Nelson Doubleday. And yet even in my day, long before the Wilpons took over the team, former players didn't really pass through our clubhouse the way they did, say, at Yankee Stadium, or the way they did when I played in Oakland, where those great A's teams of the 1970s were treated like royalty.

This meant that if you were a student of the game and you were playing or broadcasting for the Mets, you had to do a lot of your studying away from the field. And you had to take your brushes-with-greatness where you could find them, because you just didn't get the same opportunities to connect with these old-timers at Shea Stadium or Citi Field as you might have if you were toiling in any other ballpark, for any other team.

Willie Mays, Duke Snider, Warren Spahn, Richie Ashburn . . . a lot of these all-time greats who might have had their all-time greatest years elsewhere never really passed through Shea during my playing days. This was, and remains, a shame. Of course, there were exceptions—**Yogi Berra** among them. Yogi wasn't exactly a fixture in our clubhouse, but he was an occasional presence, especially during his famous feud with George Steinbrenner when he vowed never to set foot in Yankee Stadium. Happily, Yogi had some serious Shea pedigree—he'd finished his playing career with a couple cameo appearances for the Mets in 1965, and managed the team during its storied run to the 1973 World Series—so he got his baseball fix across town, where he was always welcome.

My favorite Yogi memory found me away from the stadium, though, and I'm afraid it's not the most flattering. It's a memory my son Jordan would like to forget—and I suspect someday, after years of therapy, he will. We were playing in Yogi's golf tournament out in New Jersey. Jordan was maybe eight or nine years old at the time. It wasn't one of those father-son tournaments, where you might expect to see a lot of kids in tow, but Jordan was a terrific golfer, more than able to hold his own in our foursome. I was only too happy to be able to bring him along with me. At lunch, Yogi came and sat at our table, and told every story under the moon. Jordan was like a pig in shit—he was a mad baseball fan back then, so he drank these stories in. As his father, it was a wonderful thing to see him so connected to my world in this way, and to the men who helped to make my world what it was. It was pretty cool, too, to see him out on the golf course, smacking the hell out of the ball, and pushing us oldsters around—he actually won a couple holes, as I recall.

It was only after our round that Jordan's age began to show. He was confident as hell about his ability, but a little shy about some of the other aspects of the game—specifically, about being in the locker room with a bunch of strangers. I can understand that now, although I wasn't thinking along these lines at the time. It had been a ridiculously hot day, and our shirts were soaked through, so I insisted Jordan hit the showers before we sat down for the dinner and drinks portion of the event. I'd brought along a change of clothes for him, wanted him to look presentable.

He said, "Dad, I'm not taking a shower with all these old guys." Like, there was no way in hell.

I said, "Jordan, it was a hundred degrees out there. You're all sweaty. We've got to clean up before dinner." Like he was absolutely going to listen to his father on this.

He said, "It makes no sense for me to shower and put on the same sweaty clothes." Like he wasn't going down without a fight.

I showed him the nice clean clothes I'd brought for him to wear to dinner—clean socks and underwear, too!

He said, "Dad!" He said it in that voice kids use when they've run out of argument but want to put it out there that there's just . . . one . . . more . . . thing—a *thing* he couldn't quite put into words.

I might be a dumb jock, but I'm not an idiot, so I finally figured it out. Naturally, Jordan was embarrassed to walk around naked in the locker room with all these guys, so I brought him back to see that the shower stalls were curtained in a way that he could have his privacy. After a while, Jordan got comfortable with the idea, and when he was good to go I handed him his clean clothes and he disappeared behind the curtain to do his thing.

It was when he was finished that he came full in the face with an image that continues to haunt him. There, in the next stall, completely naked, behind no curtain at all, was our host. And he wasn't just standing there. No, he was bending over to pick up a bar of soap—as in a cliché, or the punch line to an unfortunate joke. (Or, as it happens, the crux of a classic Robert Klein bit, in which the comedian and lifelong baseball fan talked about "the great trauma and privilege of seeing Yogi Berra naked.") Poor Jordan couldn't turn his head in time to avoid the crack of Yogi Berra's ass—oh, man . . . he got a real eyeful.

It's an image that continues to terrify Jordan, all these years later—and after hearing his description, I was never again able to sit and chat with Yogi without cracking a smile.

One of the great side benefits to my role as a broadcaster is the chance it offers to meet some of the visiting dignitaries of the game. When you're working in a major market like New York, that can sometimes mean you're visited by big stars from beyond the world of baseball—Broadway performers, local politicians, celebrities with movies or products or causes to promote.

That's what happened one night in the SNY booth when we were visited by **Michael Milken**, the junk bond financier who'd famously pled guilty to securities violations back during my playing days. After serving his time, Milken turned his attention to philanthropy, and for a number of years he'd partnered with Major League Baseball to promote prostate cancer awareness. Milken's interest came from a personal place: he'd been diagnosed soon after his release, and was now in remission, and he spent a good chunk of each baseball season visiting ballparks around the country and talking about prostate health, sometimes teaming up with baseball veterans with their own connections to this type of cancer.

It was a good cause, and we were always happy to shine a light on Milken's effort—but I never liked the guy. I applauded what he was doing in this area, and his other good works, but I hated what he stood for back in the 1980s and could never look past his transgressions. Still, I never wanted to get in the way of one of these public service appeals, so each year when he'd come by the booth to talk about the amount of money his foundation was donating to cancer research with every big league home run hit, or whatever the tie-in was that year, I'd step out to get a cup of coffee or stretch my legs. I didn't make a big deal of it, just quietly slipped away and let him do his thing.

This one year, Milken was making the rounds with a venerable former manager, one of the great characters of the game, which led to another unflattering story—and I share it here to offer the full flavor of the not-so-glamorous life of a baseball color analyst, and the sad ways we sometimes coax our baseball legends from their homes into a spotlight that might have become a little too harsh for them. I ducked out of the booth and left these guys to make their pitch over the next half-inning, offering my chair to the former manager as I left as a way to kind of cover up my distaste for Milken. When I returned to take my seat to start the next inning, I discovered it was soaking wet. Sad to say, our visitor couldn't control his bladder and had pissed all over my chair.

It wasn't the poor guy's fault, of course. And I'm betting/hoping he wasn't even aware he'd had an accident. But the discovery set in motion this ridiculous comedy of errors: first, nobody could find a replacement chair, so I had to call the whole rest of the game while standing up. Next, after one of our assistants had wheeled the chair away, presumably out of the booth, we noticed it had merely been pushed to the corner. After it was wheeled away a second time, again presumably, we spotted it again, stuck in the opposite corner.

And then, sure enough, there it was again the next afternoon, as we filed into the booth to go over our notes for the pregame, wheeled right back to its usual spot, pressed beneath the counter, looking out onto the field—still soaking wet from the night before.

Try as we might, we couldn't get rid of that chair. It kept coming back! Like it was haunted! A living, breathing reminder that we should each make an appointment to get our prostates checked.

Jordan was with me for another close encounter with another big league manager—Tigers skipper **Sparky Anderson**. We were up in Cooperstown for this one. Dennis Eckersley had invited me up to join him for his Hall of Fame induction ceremony, and I brought Jordan along to get another glimpse of baseball history—appropriately clad, I hoped.

At a dinner the night before the ceremony, we ran into Sparky, who couldn't have been nicer to Jordan.

Sparky mussed Jordan's hair—said, "How you doin', little guy?"

Jordan was used to having his hair mussed by these ballplayer-types, so he took it in stride, but Sparky wasn't done with him just yet. Sparky seemed to want to tell Jordan a little bit about his old man, which I thought was very generous of him—still do. He said, "I can remember the first time I saw your dad play."

He went into this long, elaborate story of a doubleheader Yale had played against Purdue, at the Tiger Town complex in Lakeland, Florida. Ruly Carpenter, the owner of the Phillies, was a Yale alum, and he used to arrange for us to come down to Florida every spring for a preseason trip. We spent most of our time in Clearwater, where the Phillies trained, and where they eventually established a minor league franchise. Sparky had just started managing the Tigers, after steering the Cincinnati Reds to a couple World Series championships, and he'd come by the stadium to take in these games—and now, more than twenty years later, he remembered them like they'd been played just a couple days earlier.

I'd had no idea Sparky was even in the ballpark that day, and here he was telling Jordan how I'd thrown a four-hit shutout and stroked a couple doubles in the opener, and then came back to hit a couple home runs and a couple more doubles in the second game. He said, "He played shortstop, your old man. Did you know he used to play short?"

I remembered that doubleheader, of course. It had been a magical day. But to hear a guy like Sparky Anderson recite those line scores all these years later made it even more special—really, Sparky was just so terrific about it, so generous with his memory.

Jordan was listening intently, his eyes agog, and my heart fairly filled.

When the moment passed and Sparky moved on to share his deep well of baseball history with another lucky someone at the dinner, Jordan turned to me and said, "Who was that old guy?"

Sparky wasn't that old at the time—about fifty—but he'd had that shock of white hair since he was a relatively young man. I said, "That was Sparky Anderson, used to manage the Detroit Tigers. And he's not as old as he looks."

Jordan thought about that some, and was soon distracted by someone or something else at the dinner.

Later that night, he turned the conversation back to Sparky—said, "That stuff about that Yale doubleheader. How much of that did he get right?"

I said, "Every single thing."

Jordan said, "No way."

Way.

A couple footnotes to that "wasted" season with the Tidewater Tides. The first takes me back to Jack Aker. We ran into each other years later, after he had been out of the game a good long while and I was working as a broadcaster. And get this—he couldn't have been nicer! He even made like he was glad to see me.

I couldn't understand it, but then I thought about it, some, and it started to become clear. Absolutely, Jack Aker could have done a little more to make me feel welcome down in Tidewater. He could have found a way to connect with me over . . . *something*. But he probably had an entirely different perspective on that season as a hardened old baseball veteran than I did as a soft baseball newbie. It's likely he was just doing his job, which was to keep track of the very many moving parts that find you as the manager of a Triple-A ball club, with players coming and going all season long, and to somehow find a way to win a bunch of ball games.

It probably never even occurred to him to hold my hand, or to smooth the way for any of his players.

The second footnote was that I went home at the end of that first year in Tidewater and wanted to hang it up. I hadn't pitched all that well, hadn't made a whole lot of progress, didn't see signing on to a life of being treated so shabbily by my supposed superiors. That first year in Tulsa, I'd been shunned by my teammates, which was about what I'd expected, and now here in Tidewater I'd been shunned by my manager—and de facto pitching coach—which was not at all what I'd expected. So I went back home and said to my father, "I don't want this. This is nonsense."

My plan was to apply to law school. Or business school. Or to get a job where I could hopefully excel and people wouldn't treat me like shit—not exactly a plan, I now see, but there were a lot of different ways I could lean, once I leaned away from baseball.

My father had a different plan in mind. He said, "We don't really quit around here."

I was thinking, *Yeah, tell me something I don't already know.* But I pushed back just the same—said, "I'm not having any fun."

He said, "We'll worry about *fun* later." Like he was holding the word out in front of him so he wouldn't have to smell it.

Later that first night after I'd returned home, my father sought me out to continue the conversation—said, "Look, I know you have options. And I know you're smart enough to realize that playing this game to the best of your ability is something you not only owe to yourself, but to this ball club that just traded for you." He went on to tell me that I'd made a commitment to the game, and that I needed to honor that commitment—at least until I could look myself in the mirror and know I'd given baseball my best shot.

"Not just *a* shot," he clarified, "but the right shot."

I thought about this conversation a lot that winter, and as I thought about it my dad was working behind the scenes, doing this little mind-trick he had where he would get you in shape or in the right frame of mind to face a difficult challenge—only you'd never know he was working you over in this way. He could be a great manipulator, my dad. In this case, he had me playing racquetball. Lots and lots of racquetball. He'd just taken up the game, had made himself into one of the best players in the area in his age group, and he'd take me to the gym with him every afternoon and spank me up and down the court for a couple hours. Oh, man . . . he schooled me! Sometimes, one or more of my brothers would come along, but I was out there every day, taking my lumps in this regimented way.

I was putting in a ton of other work at the gym, too. I was lifting, running . . . eating right. But mostly I was doing these things so I could stand up to my father on the court, never really thinking about stepping up my game and getting in shape for spring training. It was about getting quicker and stronger, so I could compete with my dad. It was about pushing myself to get better. It was about trusting the process—that's a line my father started using on me. It was a military thing, he said. I had only to give myself over to the process to achieve the desired result.

"Trust the process," he started to say, at some midpoint during the off-season.

And so I began to trust the process. I had no idea I was being coached, no idea I was being manipulated by this man who only wanted the best for me—who only wanted me to discover the best in myself. In my mind, I was just passing the time, hanging out with my dad, figuring out some kind of next move. In his mind, he was giving me the space to get my mind right and my body right, and to put that dispiriting Tidewater season behind me.

By the end of the winter, I could pretty much keep up with my father on the racquetball court. And somewhere in there I had pretty much come to the determination that the life I was living that winter in Millbury, Massachusetts, wasn't the life I wanted for myself. I'd go out with my friends some nights and roll in at two or three or four o'clock in the morning, just as I'd hear my father getting ready to start his day. He was out the door every morning at four-thirty for work. He lived a disciplined life, and it was a good life, but it wasn't for me. Understand, I hadn't really lived in my parents' house for any length of time since I'd gone off to college, so this was a revelation to me, the life that was waiting for me in this town, in this house, in my old room.

Without really realizing it, without really meaning to, I'd gotten myself into shape to face another baseball season.

Without really realizing it, without really meaning to, I'd come to a decision. I would report to spring training that February and work like crazy to put myself in position to take that shot my father talked to me about—not just *a* shot, but the right shot.

Because, hey, I wasn't done with the game just yet.

9

In the Booth

I was only dimly aware of the Mets' broadcasting history when I joined the team in 1983, although I understood full well the impact a long-tenured announcer could have on a ball club and its community of fans. As a lifelong New Englander, I'd grown up listening to the legendary **Ned Martin**, who was known for his signature exclamation—"Mercy!"—as well as his tendency to quote Shakespeare or Updike, just to keep us Red Sox fans on our toes.

As Boston fans of a certain age will surely remember, Ned Martin replaced the also-legendary **Curt Gowdy**, who'd been the voice of the team for fifteen years before leaving to do his thing on the national stage for NBC Sports. I was only five years old when Gowdy called his last game as a Red Sox announcer, so I have no firsthand memories of his time with the locals, but every time he came on to call the *Game of the Week* someone would invariably remark how he'd been one of ours, so the connection was always made clear.

Ned Martin's voice is the one that attaches to my boyhood memories of my beloved Sox, just as it does for my brothers, and anyone else who came of baseball age in that part of the world in the late 1960s, in time to tap into those Yaz-fueled teams that took us (at last!) to a couple World Series. There's a famous story about Ned Martin's death that belongs in these pages for the way it reinforces his lifelong connection to this team and its rich history. In 2002, at the age of seventy-eight, he traveled to Boston from Virginia to attend the funeral of the apparently mortal Ted Williams, who had been the face of the Red Sox since 1939. It was only fitting that the voice of the franchise pay his respects to the face of the franchise, right? But while he was returning to Virginia the following day, Ned Martin suffered a fatal heart attack on a shuttle bus at the Raleigh-Durham International Airport, suggesting to the legion of Boston's faithful fans, not yet known as Red Sox Nation, that the heartache they all felt over the passing of "Teddy Ball game" was all too real.

The Mets had their own rich history on the broadcasting front, but it took me a while to appreciate it. The team was famous for its rotating trio of announcers—***Ralph Kiner***, ***Bob Murphy***, and ***Lindsey Nelson***, who traded off duties on radio and television. For seventeen years, this group stayed together, from Day One of the Mets' inaugural season, through the team's unlikely "worst to first" run to the 1969 World Series, all the way to 1979 when Lindsey Nelson left the team to call games for the San Francisco Giants. It was Lindsey Nelson who was the star of that group at the outset, and even though it turned out to be one of the longest-running teams in the game, with an equal division of labor, he was meant to be the lead broadcaster because he was the one with years of experience. Ralph Kiner only had a single season in the booth, working for the Chicago White Sox the year before, and Bob Murphy had a stint alongside Curt Gowdy in the Red Sox booth for a couple seasons before calling games for the Baltimore Orioles for two seasons, replacing the great Ernie Harwell.

But it was Ralph Kiner who turned out to be the team's enduring star—in part, because of his longevity, but mostly because of his deep well of knowledge and transparent affection for the game and the hopelessly young team he was assigned to cover. (Or, perhaps I should say the *haplessly* young team he was assigned to cover—those first couple Mets teams were historically lousy!) He called games for the Mets until his death, at the age of ninety-one, capping an incredible fifty-three seasons as a broadcaster, which in turn capped his own Hall of Fame career as one of the game's preeminent sluggers. He was also beloved for his malapropisms. He was famous for screwing up people's names, including his own. For years, he called Gary Carter "Gary Cooper," and his eventual colleague **Tim McCarver** was often introduced as "Tim MacArthur." But Met fans didn't care—they took his point, and Ralph really knew his stuff, even if he didn't always sweat the details.

Once, after Tim McCarver joined the broadcast team, the Mets were in St. Louis for a game against the Cardinals, when a young right-hander named **Brent Gaff** was called on to pitch. I'd played with Brent in Tidewater, and shortly after I was called up on September 1, 1983, he got his own September nod. The guys in production had made sure to let Ralph and Tim know this kid's backstory, because it offered the kind of detail that made the game more personal. In those days, covering another dreadful Mets team, the production office was always looking for ways to keep things interesting. The hook here was that Brent Gaff was from Fort Wayne, Indiana, and he had family all over the Midwest, and they were all Cardinals fans. He had about sixty people out at the stadium to watch him pitch, and they were all rooting for him against their hometown team. It was a good story line— the kind of thing the folks at home love to hear.

Well, Ralph told the hell out of Brent Gaff's backstory as he came into the game, but he never got around to saying his name. Ralph talked about Indiana, about the sixty tickets he left for friends and family, about how he'd grown up cheering for the Cardinals. Finally, the drum roll complete, he introduced the Mets rookie . . . as *Brent Frank*.

This alone wouldn't have been so remarkable, because Ralph was known for botching players' names, even in midcareer—it was one of his signature charms. It's what happened next that turned the moment from the merely ridiculous to the sublime, and what happened next was that Tim took out a piece of paper and scribbled a correction. Evidently, these gaffes happened frequently enough that they had a system worked out to set things right.

He wrote: *Gaff*.

In the retelling, it would appear that the "system" they'd worked out didn't account for a pitcher with a name that at first glance might have also signaled a mistake of some kind.

Ralph, quick on his feet, went into his version of auto correct mode. He apologized to the folks at home, explained how it can sometimes get confusing for an old-timer like himself, with all these players coming and going this time of year, said he'd made a mistake. Then he introduced the kid pitcher a second time— saying, "Now pitching, for the New York Mets . . . *Frank Gaff*."

This time, Timmy didn't bother to correct him, probably on the learned truth that this was close enough.

• • •

im McCarver was one of the best in the business. He joined the Mets the same year I did—him up in the booth, me up on the mound. As far as I ever knew, he and Ralph were the primary voices of the team on the television side. Bob Murphy was the lead voice on the radio side, paired at first with Gary Thorne—and then, toward the end of my time in New York, with **Gary Cohen**, my eventual partner when I started broadcasting games for the Mets in 2006.

A lot of the guys who used to work with Tim often tell me how serious he was when he first took the Mets job—and how Ralph would try to loosen him up. Tim himself used to tell me that partnering with Ralph was the best thing that could have happened to him as a broadcaster, because it showed him the importance of lightness and laughter in calling a game. The two of them used to talk about this type of thing on the air, during a lull in the action. Tim would talk about the grind of the long baseball season, and Ralph would shoot back and say, "What do you know about the grind of the long baseball season? You never played every day."

This was only partly true. Early on in Timmy's playing career, which ran from 1959 to 1980 (covering four decades!), he was the Cardinals' primary catcher. He even finished second in the National League MVP voting in 1967, the year the Cardinals won the World Series, so he was certainly an impact player for a stretch. However, during the back-half of his career, he was mostly a backup catcher—and he's probably best remembered for his role as the exclusive catcher of future Hall of Famer Steve Carlton.

Ralph was always putting Timmy in his place like that—and Ralph was such a favorite of the Mets' fan base by that point Timmy knew he couldn't push back in anything more than a halfhearted way. It would be like lashing out at everyone's favorite uncle over Christmas dinner.

One of Ralph's best lines, which he took to trotting out with more and more frequency as his time in the booth grew longer and longer, was another way to remind Tim and the listeners at home that he was once one of the game's most feared hitters, leading the league in home runs in each of his first seven seasons with the Pirates.

The line: "Home run hitters drive Cadillacs. Singles hitters drive Fords."

This was mostly true. Ralph said it first during his playing days, and it got a lot of attention, and it found its way into the broadcast from time to time—like one of his greatest hits! He'd been at this Mets job since just about forever, so I think Ralph sometimes fretted that the fans no longer remembered him as a player. This was mostly true as well, but only because Ralph hung around the game for so long that most of the folks who'd seen him play were dead and gone. And so let the record show that for a while in there he was a true rock star of the game—a real ladies' man, too. He used to date Elizabeth Taylor, and Ava Gardner, and Raquel Welch, and a host of other beautiful starlets. A great many of those celebrity-driven dalliances came about because Bing Crosby was a part-owner of the Pirates during Ralph's playing days, and according to Ralph he was very good at orchestrating all these photo opportunities for the gossip columnists and newsreels of the day. It was good for business, Bing Crosby used to say, for the Pirates players to be seen out and about with these beautiful women on their arms, and Ralph was only too happy to comply.

Still, it was hard for those of us who knew Ralph as this avuncular presence to reconcile the baseball lifer he'd become with the man about town he certainly was, but let the record also show that he was an impeccable dresser, in his day, and one of the game's most eligible bachelors—and I'm sure the Cadillac all those home runs entitled him to drive didn't hurt!

We'd try to press him for details on his love life during his bachelor days, but he was always such a gentleman . . . *on the air.* Between innings, or after-hours, we could sometimes get him to loosen up, but one of my favorite stories to come out of Ralph's "dating" career found us in the 1986 season. We were in the clubhouse after a game in Philly. The actress Jamie Lee Curtis was in town with her husband, Christopher Guest, and the two stopped in for a visit. Ralph knew they were coming by and came down to say hello, and in his charming, chivalrous way he mentioned to Jamie Lee that he had once dated her mother.

With perfect comic timing, Jamie Lee waited a beat and then jumped into Ralph's arms and shouted, "Daddy!"

During the Mets' final season at Shea Stadium, in 2008, conversation in the booth would often turn to the ballpark's rich history—it was a way to fill the time, and to reminisce. As it happened, Ralph was at his best as a broadcaster when he was encouraged to share an old story from his playing days, or an observation about a long-dead player, or a years-ago promotion at Shea. Gary Cohen remarked one night how the ballpark had hosted every type of event over the years, from a Beatles concert to the Ice Capades.

Ralph, well into his eighties by this point, seemed to pick up at this mention of the Ice Capades, and he allowed enthusiastically that he'd once hosted an Ice Capades event when he was the general manager of the San Diego Padres of the Pacific Coast League, at Westgate Park. At first, we all thought we were caught inside one of Ralph's malapropisms or *misrememberings,* because his comment made no sense. The Ice Capades? At an outdoor stadium in

Southern California? It just didn't seem possible, so after the game Gary brought it up again.

He said, "The Ice Capades, in San Diego? How did that work, exactly?"

Ralph explained it in such a way that left Gary and me to think he might be conflating one memory with another, which often happened at that stage in Ralph's career. However, we also knew Ralph well enough to know that he'd get around to making his point eventually. With Ralph, it often worked out that what came across as far-fetched was . . . well, merely *fetched*. His memory was far more sound than it might have appeared, so we waited for the essence of the story to become clear.

After a while, with clarity nowhere in sight, Gary started looking for a way to help Ralph dig himself out of the hole he seemed to have made for himself. He said, "Forget how you managed to pull it off. How did you even sell tickets? Who's going to see the Ice Capades in San Diego?"

Ralph said, "Are you kidding me? Have you ever seen the asses on those skaters? We sold those tickets in no time."

As it turned out, Ralph used to date Sonja Henie, the Norwegian figure skater, so at least we knew he wasn't talking out of his own ass on this one.

I never really knew Lindsey Nelson, from the Mets' original broadcasting trio—he of the famously loud and arguably stylish sports jackets that used to leave viewers at home scrambling to adjust the color on their sets. He'd moved on by the time I joined the team, and only visited the ballpark infrequently during my playing days, but Bob Murphy was the radio voice of the team throughout my time in New York—he probably called every single game I ever pitched in a Mets uniform.

Murph had a tremendous voice, and a poetic streak. He used to
like to pepper his commentary with the kind of ten-dollar words
that left listeners reaching for their dictionaries. He also used to
like his cocktails, and here I think it helps to understand that
drinking had always been a big part of the game's culture. This is
not me calling Bob Murphy out. This is me telling it like it was.
Ballplayers drank. The managers and coaches drank. The broadcasters and sportswriters who covered the team all drank. In a lot
of ways, a life in the game was one giant party, and on this one
trip to Houston it appeared that Murph had tied on a few too many.

To be clear, it wasn't just *any* trip to Houston. It was *the* trip to
Houston—to open the 1986 playoff series against the Astros. In
those days, at the Astrodome, you had to take a bus to get to the
stadium. You couldn't catch a cab from the hotel, because they
wouldn't let you into the complex—it was so damn huge. They'd
have to let you off a few hundred yards from the entrance, so a large
group of us arrived together on a bus that had been arranged for
the team.

We walked into the clubhouse, en masse, and there on the trainer's table was Bob Murphy, out cold.

Now, we'd all seen Murph drunk before, we'd all seen each other
drunk, so the sight of Bob Murphy splayed out on the trainer's table
didn't even rate a double take. What was strange, looking back,
was the setting. You have to realize, in most big league clubhouses,
the trainer's table was too small for us players to do anything but
sit on it. We'd use it to get our ankles taped, or maybe to sit down
while one of the trainers worked on our shoulders. But you hardly
ever saw someone lying down on the trainer's table—that is, unless
you were Bob Murphy, who happened to be short enough to fit,
and who also happened to be completely shit-faced.

Still, we had a game to get ready for, a big game, so nobody paid attention to poor Murph. We just went about our business, like he wasn't even there. We even gathered around the trainer's table for a team meeting. We weren't in the habit on that '86 team of holding a lot of team meetings—that just wasn't Davey Johnson's way—but this was the first game of a big playoff series, and we wanted to get things off on the right note. Plus, there was a Major League Baseball representative on hand to walk us through the plan for the opening ceremonies, so there were a few logistics to go over as well. Trouble was, there was no suitable place in the visitor's clubhouse for the entire team to gather, so we just stood around the trainer's table and went over whatever it was we had to go over . . . the whole time, standing *over* Murph, who was laid out like the guest of honor at a wake.

Sadly, weirdly, hilariously, the meeting went on as if Bob Murphy was the centerpiece at a fine buffet table, and as the meeting was breaking up, somebody finally acknowledged the proverbial *elephant in the room* and said something about Murph's condition. Might have been another player, or one of our clubhouse guys, but at some point somebody said, "By the way, what the hell is wrong with Murph?"

Davey Johnson, who'd been running the meeting, took it on himself to answer. He said, "The doctors are on their way. We think Murph had a stroke."

He said this without missing a beat, as if the fact that the team's longtime radio announcer was passed out in the middle of the room had been discussed and carefully considered by the powers that be.

Of course, we'd been around long enough to know that a "stroke" was a euphemism for being blackout drunk, and that there were no doctors en route, so we let the comment sink in, and then after another while, someone asked what time we were supposed to take BP.

That's the kind of team we were—this venerable broadcaster was passed out on the trainer's table, dead to the world, and all we cared about was when we were going to hit.

I t's been one of the great blessings of my baseball life to work with **Keith Hernandez** and **Gary Cohen**. We've got a good thing going, and one of the reasons for that, I think, is that we all love the game and share a deep affection for the Mets organization and for each other.

If that sounds corny . . . well, pass the salt. If it doesn't . . . well, I guess that means you're a regular viewer.

Another reason for our long-running success is the way we've been encouraged to talk about our lives away from the ballpark, and to share our thoughts and observations with the fans in ways that make it feel like we're calling these games over beers. We might spend a couple minutes talking about the long line at the Shake Shack concession out in center field, or the U.S. Open tennis championships being played next door to Citi Field, or the latest summer blockbuster movie. Everything is up for discussion in our broadcasts—there's room for shtick and analysis, and that's what the fans are responding to.

For example, Keith and Gary talk all the time about cartoons. It's amazing to me how many times the subject comes up on our air—and what's equally amazing is how much these two know about cartoons. I've taken to calling them "The Latchkey Kids," because when they get going on this I start to wonder if they came home from school every day and planted themselves in front of the television until dinner. Think about it: we're all about the same age, so we should share some of the same pop culture references, but I have no idea what these guys are talking about half the time. *Tom & Jerry, Bugs Bunny, The Flintstones* . . . sure, I know all of that. But these guys can do a deep dive down the rabbit hole from time to time, and I've got no idea where they're headed.

When they throw to me, I'll say something like, "Did either one of you ever read a book when you were a kid?"

We hear from our viewers all the time that watching the Mets with us is like tuning in to a talk show—and, curiously, that there are a bunch of well-established drinking games that have sprouted up around our broadcasts. Forget the Nielsen ratings or the other more traditional metrics we use to measure who's watching. What it comes down to, in the end, is the number of drinking games in place in support of what you're doing—it's the Bottoms Up, Bottom Line indicator of how many people are watching and how they're responding. Keith always loves to talk about "the Cardinal way," or to slip in a reverent reference to the great Lou Brock, so each time he does you're supposed to take a drink. With Gary, it's every time he mentions Columbia University, his alma mater. With me, I never mention Yale in the broadcast—an affectation that comes from years of trying to play down my educational background with my teammates—but whenever Yale comes up, you take a shot.

And on and on.

Lately, I've started to think that one of the things we've got to get better at, if we mean to grow our "game" and keep our broadcasts relevant, is extending our pop culture reach. We need to start talking about things that might connect with our younger viewers, or we'll start to sound like a bunch of curmudgeons. For example, during a recent lull in the game, we started talking about our plans for the weekend. I happened to mention that I had tickets to see the great EDM deejay Steve Aoki at this club in New York. I don't think Keith or Gary had any idea who I was talking about, but the kids in the truck, working the broadcast, were whispering in my headphones—saying, "Oh, my God, RJ! That's so awesome. You mentioned Aoki!"

We need to do more of that. We need to make our references younger, smarter, more contemporary.

We enjoy the hell out of each other during the games, but as soon as the final out is made we can't wait to get out of there. Keith has this briefcase he always carries, and he'll start to pack up his notes and his scorebook as we head into the ninth inning so he can snap the thing closed and make for the exits at first chance. The thing of it is, when we're at home, it's tough to leave the ballpark without running past a gauntlet of fans who want to stop and grab an autograph or a selfie, maybe talk about the game.

One of the things the fans don't realize is that we're not just eager to leave the ballpark—we've had enough of each other, too. When you're on the air together for four hours, talking baseball and riffing on this and that, the last thing you want to do is go out for a drink or to dinner. Of course, there are exceptions to this general rule—like this one time when we were in Philadelphia and Keith and I decided to stop at the hotel bar for a glass of wine. We sat down and drank our wine, but after a couple minutes I turned to Keith and said, "Okay, I'm good. That's enough for me."

Keith said, "Yeah, me, too. I'm done."

As we headed upstairs to our rooms, we stepped into an elevator with two middle-aged Mets fans. One was wearing a Jose Reyes jersey and the other was wearing a David Wright jersey, so it was a safe bet that they knew who we were and why we were in town.

It made sense—Philly was just a couple hours' drive from New York, so a lot of fans would make the trip, maybe even make a weekend out of it.

Keith looked these guys up and down, and I just knew he was about to say something. They looked to be about the same age as us—fifty to sixty, somewhere in there.

Sure enough, Keith couldn't leave it alone. He said, "Excuse me, but how fucking old are you guys?"

They mentioned their ages and Keith said, "Aren't you a little old to be wearing baseball jerseys?"

The two guys didn't say anything.

Keith didn't say anything.

I didn't say anything.

Keith's comment just kind of hung there, as the elevator did its thing. Finally, the doors opened onto Keith's floor and he stepped out, leaving me in the cab with Jose Reyes and David Wright— thinking, *This is going to be awkward.*

And it was, until I could see Reyes turn to Wright in my peripheral vision and give him a high five. Then I heard him say, "That was fucking awesome," and they started clapping each other on the back like they'd just made some game-winning play.

I turned and said good night to these guys when we got to my floor and I realized that Keith was probably the only guy I knew who could get away with something like that. I mean, if I'd called these guys out on their jerseys they would have thought I was an arrogant prick. I would have become "that asshole Ron Darling" in the punch line to their story. But with Keith, he can be sweet and sour all at once, and the fans just love that about him. They love that he doesn't suffer fools gladly, and that he feels free to call them out on their shit.

He's one of them . . . and it's a great, good thing.

Gary's the glue of our broadcast, of course. He's the best play-by-play guy working today—certainly the best *I've* ever worked with. I can't imagine anyone was ever better. I admire the hell out of what he can do behind his mic. I admire the hell out of the career he's made for himself, out of nothing at all. What a lot of folks don't realize is how difficult it is to make it on the broadcasting side of the baseball business if you aren't a former player. You've got to beat the bushes, calling games in out-of-the-way places, for little to no money, in venues where there are sometimes more players on the field than there are people in the stands. And yet he left Columbia and went off in pursuit of his dreams, working in Pawtucket and Durham and all these other small, minor league towns, logging the time. The progression is tough, straightforward: you go from Low A to High A, Double-A to Triple-A, and when you get your shot, you've got to find a way to stick. And for Gary to be a Queens kid, growing up wearing #3 on his Little League jersey to honor his favorite player, Bud Harrelson, to be calling Mets games, first on radio and now on television, it's like he's died and gone to heaven.

His first love is radio, and you can hear that love in his voice as he paints the scene of each game. He speaks in full, clear sentences. His anecdotes and asides are peppered with history, sincerity, integrity. He's the caretaker of Mets legend and lore, and what's great about the club's broadcasting setup is that Gary's got a full counterpart in this in **Howie Rose** on the radio side—two guys with a face for radio (forgive, please, the too-easy jab), and a heart for their beloved Metsies and the game itself that knows no bounds.

With Gary, I regard him as such royalty I have a hard time busting his chops, and what's amazing to me are the stories he tells of when he was pounding the pavement, trying to get people in the business to listen to his tapes, applying for this or that job, clawing his way up the ladder, while all these so-called experts were telling him he didn't have what it took to make it. What the hell were these people listening to? How is it possible that such abundant talent could have been so easily overlooked? The one knock on Gary, early on, was that he spoke with a Queens accent, and I don't know this part of the story from Gary, but Keith once told me that Gary actually went to a vocal coach to get rid of some of the local *patois*—that's how determined he was to succeed.

One thing about Gary: like a lot of New York–born broadcasters of a certain age, he grew up listening to **Marv Albert**, the longtime voice of the Knicks and Rangers. In baseball, we always talk about these legendary managers whose coaches inevitably graduate to managerial careers of their own. We talk about the Scioscia effect or the Maddon effect. Well, in broadcasting, there's an equally long line of talented broadcasters who are in the booth because of the Albert effect, and Gary stands at the head of that long line.

Someday, soon, people will be talking about the Gary Cohen effect—hopefully, with a Queens accent.

My partners in the booth extend far beyond Citi Field, and I've been blessed during my time calling national games for TBS to share the microphone with three Hall of Famers I now get to call teammates.

I've got a story to tell about each . . .

Frank Thomas was the best hitter in baseball for a good chunk of his career—they didn't call him "The Big Hurt" for nothing—but I only got to face him during my last couple seasons, when I didn't have a whole lot of ways to get him out. The knock on Frank, even early on in his career, was that he was always pulling the baseball equivalent of a flop, in hopes of getting a call from the home plate umpire. He was famous among opposing pitchers for the way he'd jump back, almost out of the box, on any pitch that was even remotely inside—and, as often as not, he'd get the call. What this meant for me and my fellow pitchers was that we couldn't really pitch him inside. That spot on the inside corner that would usually belong to me for a strike? It belonged to Frank, and it pissed me off.

Just how much it pissed me off seemed to come to the surface on an August night in Oakland during my first full season with the A's. We were making a push for the playoffs, and I was still feeling my way around the league. I'd had some success against Frank, first few times I'd faced him—but then, he'd had some success against me, as well. Not on this night, though. I'd gotten him out on a couple grounders and a popup to second, when he came up to face me for the fourth time—runners on first and third, one out. We were up 5–3 in the top of the eighth, and I'd only thrown about a hundred pitches to this point in the game, so Tony La Russa left me in to clean up my own mess.

Frank cut an intimidating figure when he strode to the plate, especially when he represented the winning run, but as I stared him down all I could see was a big ol' baby. Yeah, he was six-foot-five, built like the football player he was back in college, an incredible hitter, but to me he was just a major league pussy, the way he always cried to the ump for that call inside—oh, man, I hated that shit. I'd think, *Are you kidding me? This guy played tight end at Auburn?* But here it worked out that I threw a 2–0 pitch that ran inside on him at the last minute, and he could only fist it on the ground to short for a 6–4–3 double play to get me out of the inning.

Frank was pissed! He threw his bat down as he ran to first and he started *motherfucking* me on his way to the bag. I pretended not to hear him—said, "What was that, Frank? You got something to say?"

He turned to me and shouted, "You're lucky I didn't hit that ball five hundred feet."

We went back and forth for another few beats, as my teammates left the field, and while Frank was still in earshot I fired off my last salvo—said, "I didn't just get *you* out, motherfucker! You made *two* outs, so fuck you!"

(Happily, they didn't mic the players in those days!)

Dennis Eckersley, our Cy Young Award–winning closer (and MVP!), came on in the ninth to put the game away for us for his 37th save of the season, on his way to a league-leading total of 51, and that was that.

I'd go on to face Frank Thomas a few times more in my career, and for the most part he had my number—other than this one 0–4 night in Oakland, he beat me up at a .437 clip, going 7-for-16 against me. But I don't think we exchanged words until we met again as colleagues, when we were both working the playoffs for TBS, and here again I wasn't shy about letting Frank know what I thought of him. Say what you will about us aging ballplayers—we have long memories. And say what you will about *this* aging ballplayer—I have zero tolerance for players who bitch and moan about nothing at all, especially when it messes with my game plan.

The thing is, once I actually got to know Frank and started working with him at Turner, I came to like him. He was a pretty good guy. He was funny, smart, personable. We got along great, even though I still carried some of the same resentments from our time on the battlefield, along with a couple new ones that had nothing to do with Frank himself and everything to do with the ways a legendary ballplayer is treated alongside the ways a somewhat-less-than-legendary ballplayer is treated.

So there I was, trying to reconcile the image I'd had of Frank as a whining giant alongside this somewhat more positive second impression that was beginning to form of Frank as a friend and colleague . . . and underneath those two images were these not-so-subtle reminders from the TBS brass that Frank was a Hall of Famer and I was not.

It was Frank's first postseason on the TBS crew, as I recall, working the pre- and postgame shift. The series I was covering had already wrapped. I was in limbo, my calendar on hold, waiting to see where I'd go next—the life of a postseason announcer. At two-thirty in the morning, the phone rang on my night table. It was Tim Kiely, who produced our pre- and postgame shows. T.K. was also the guy responsible for Turner's award-winning pre- and postgame shows for the network's NBA coverage, widely considered the best show in sports television, and here he'd been tasked with working some of that same magic on the baseball front.

He said, "Whatchya doin', Ronnie? It's T.K."

I said, "Whaddya mean, what am I doin'? It's two-thirty in the morning. I'm in bed."

He said, "Wake up, motherfucker. Our pre- and post- sucks."

I said, "Okay, but again, it's two-thirty in the morning. What do you want me to do about it?"

He said, "I've got you on a six a.m. flight. We're flying you in. Need you to work the pre- and post- until the next round. Car's coming for you at four."

I said, "I've never done pre- or post-."

He said, "I don't give a shit. You're a pro. I need you to figure out how to bring Frank into the conversation."

Frank Thomas had been doing the pre- and post- with Cal Ripken Jr. and Ernie Johnson—and T.K. was right, the show had yet to hit its stride. I certainly wasn't the solution, but Frank and Cal were still finding their voice. Me, I had a whole other year on them at TBS, which I guess made me an experienced veteran. (Plus, I was on the payroll, so T.K. and company probably just figured they'd get their money's worth.)

The way T.K. had the show set up was that each of us had our own segment. Cal did his thing, then Frank did his thing, then I did my thing—with Ernie presiding. I wasn't happy about being dragged from home on what I'd thought would be a couple days off, so I was a little on edge. As we went into a break, Frank came over to me and said, "Shit, you've got a lot of energy." For some reason, it rubbed me the wrong way. It was a nothing line, just something to say, but I went off on Frank. It wasn't my nature, and Frank certainly didn't deserve to hear from me on this, but I was pissed that I'd been called in to fill in some of the gaps for these two great players—like they were messing with my game plan all over again. They just needed to sit there and look Hall of Fameish. Me, I wasn't a great player, so I had to get out of bed at two-thirty in the morning.

I should have let Frank's comment slide, but I lit into him—same way I'd lit into him on the field that night in Oakland, when we were jawing on the field. I said, "Frank, what the fuck do you think we're doing here? This is live television. You can't just show up. You've got to bring it."

The folks in the booth, they looked at me like I'd lost a couple screws, but I didn't care. For all those years, I wasn't a big fan of Frank's, and on this night I wasn't a big fan of being there. So I let it rip.

The kicker to this story came a couple days later, when we were in Colorado to do the pregame there. Here's a learned truth about October baseball in Colorado: it can get pretty damn cold. I think it was about 25 degrees on the set, which was down on the field. I'd planned ahead and had on a jacket and scarf and gloves. Cal and Ernie were dressed for the weather as well. T.K. even arranged for Charles Barkley to "cross-over" from the basketball side and make a visit to the set to try and pump up the energy, and he was bundled up appropriately, too. But there was Frank, freezing his ass off.

Now, in fairness to Frank, it was a cold, cold night, but somehow the rest of us knew to dress for the weather. And yet because he was the great Frank Thomas, the biggest baby to ever make it to the Hall of Fame, one of the game's all-time moaners and whiners, the producers went to him after the pregame and told him to get himself a coat and charge it to the show. So he did. He went out to what had to have been the most expensive menswear store in Denver and bought himself a $12,000 mohair coat. No shit, no lie. And TBS just smiled and paid for it, while I sat there thinking, *Damn, if I'd been a little more dominant as a pitcher, if I'd bitched and moaned a little more, maybe I could have gotten a $12,000 mohair coat.*

The next Hall of Famer in the TBS lineup is **John Smoltz**. We've got different personalities, we sit on opposite sides of the political spectrum, but during the cozy confines of the game Smoltzie and I get along great. And he really knows his stuff—if they handed out graduate degrees for breadth and depth of baseball knowledge, he'd have a PhD.

During his playing days, John and the other aces in that great Braves rotation were famous for the bond they shared. Tom Glavine, Greg Maddux and them, they played golf together, had dinner together, did everything together. They were their own little fraternity. It wasn't like that with my Mets brethren. We were close, in uniform, could talk pitching with each other deep into the night, but I was very happy not to see my fellow pitchers until we got to the ballpark, and I'm sure they felt the same way about me. I wasn't close to Dwight or Sid or Coney or Bobby O or whoever else we had in our rotation—not in the way those Braves pitchers were close.

What Smoltzie shared with his fellow aces was a rare and special thing, and I think it pushed all three of them to a level of enduring greatness that seemed just out of reach for us Mets pitchers. Even the Braves' back-of-the-rotation guys, like Steve Avery and Kevin Millwood, were able to lift their games on the back of all that camaraderie. It wasn't like that with our club. Like I said, we had our own killer esprit de corps thing happening once the game was under way, but these guys were tight, tight, tight. They'd even play golf on days they were scheduled to pitch—that's how much they relished each other's company.

Our staff was the best in baseball for a stretch, but Dwight was the kingpin of our group. After his stunning first two seasons, that was the impression. He was our #1 starter, and the rest of us were #1-A, or #2, or #2-A. The Braves staff was the best in baseball for an even longer stretch, and those guys were all #1 starters, so maybe all that golf, all those dinners, all that time together away from the ballpark had something to do with it.

Cal Ripken Jr. was an icon of the game. Unlike Frank, I respected the hell out of him as an athlete and competitor. I loved the way he played. But I didn't always love working with him. You see, Cal has forgotten more about the game of baseball than most people who played the game will ever know. He lives and breathes this shit. His instincts and his insights are among the best I've ever seen or heard. But his demeanor doesn't really lend itself to live television. He's meticulous, thoughtful, circumspect—qualities that don't always come across in the booth, when you've got to think about things like timing, and moving the conversation along. Cal's thing is to think about whatever he says before he says it, but there's no time for that on-set. It's like Ralph Kiner used to always tell Tim McCarver—you've got to loosen things up in the booth, can't take things too, too seriously.

One of the key things I've learned in my time in the booth is that when you open your mouth you should say something—and not just *any* something, but something insightful, something meaningful, something to enhance the viewers' appreciation of the game. Cal's got way more insights into way more meaningful shit than yours truly, but when he opens his mouth it doesn't always come out, not straightaway. He takes a while to get around to making his point, so our timing is sometimes off. Nothing against Cal—I really like him as a person. But as colleagues, we don't seem to click. That happens sometimes. Just look at my relationship with Keith. There are a lot of things I don't like about Keith, but I love the guy. There are a lot of things I love about Cal, but we're not really friends away from the set. At least, with me and Keith, we've got chemistry on the air. There's a smooth give-and-take. Maybe it's because we played together, because we won a World Series together, because we have this rich, shared history. Cal and I don't have that. It's not his fault. It's not my fault. It's just how it is.

And yet the story I want to tell about Cal has nothing to do with our time as colleagues. It has nothing to do with me. It has to do with what is probably one of the finest, sweetest moments to ever pass between father and son on a baseball field. Now, I feel qualified to weigh in on such as this, because my father and I had a fine, sweet moment of our own, on the field at Fenway Park, before Game 4 of the 1986 World Series. The Mets were down two games to one in the series. I'd pitched well enough in the opener at Shea, but we'd come out on the short side of a 1–0 game, so it felt to me like I had the weight of our season on my young shoulders. That weight was particularly heavy on this night because the game was also a homecoming of sorts. I'd grown up as a baseball fan in the company of the Red Sox. When I closed my eyes and imagined myself a big league ballplayer, I was wearing a Boston uniform. And here on this grand stage, as I was warming up to pitch the biggest game of my life, I was surrounded by a couple hundred people in the stands who'd seen me grow up, who knew me or my family, who were variously torn between rooting for this local kid who'd made it to the World Series and for their local team which was in sniffing distance of a championship for the first time in sixty-eight years.

Warming up in the Fenway bullpen is a tough assignment for any visiting pitcher, because the bleacher fans are right on top of you, taunting you, trying to get in your head and under your skin and alongside all the nooks and crannies of emotions that make up your . . . well, your *makeup.* It can be a real mind game out there, and for me it was tougher still because of the emotional connection I'd always felt to this place, to this team, to these fans. Hell, for the first twenty-one years of my life, I was one of them, and now I was the enemy.

Perhaps because of all these mixed emotions, I had a lousy warm-up. It felt to me like I just didn't have it, couldn't hit my spots. Plus, it was cold *af,* as the young people like to say these days. My grip didn't feel right. My release was *off.* I kept throwing the ball in the dirt, and each time I did the Boston fans lit into me like I'd just shown my hand . . . which, in a way, I had.

So what did I do? Well, I cut my warm-up short. There was no point in abusing myself in this way, in front of this crowd. I told myself that either the game would find me, or I would find myself out of the game. I was resigned to it. But then, as I walked from the dugout in right field to take my spot in the Mets dugout, the most magical thing happened. I ran into my father. *On the field!* I was confused by this, at first, but then I remembered he was at the game with the Air Force Reserve, as a member of the color guard. He was on the field for the national anthem, in full dress uniform. It all came rushing back to me, as I just happened up on him.

He said, "Hey."

He wasn't much for words, my old man, but in that one word, spoken with his booming, no-bullshit voice, all the tension and uncertainty and pressure I'd been feeling during my warm-up seemed to fall away. I went from wanting to be anyplace else but on this field for this game to wanting to be nowhere else but on this field, with the man who taught me the game.

I'd been walking back to the dugout with Mel Stottlemyre, our pitching coach, but when I ran into my dad I turned to Mel and said, "I'm good, Mel. I'll hang out here in the outfield for the anthem."

Mel didn't want to leave me out in the outfield all alone like that, away from the rest of the team, but at the same time I don't think he wanted to encroach on a private family moment. So he stepped away from the two of us, and planted his feet right there in the out-field as well. And that's where we stood during the anthem—Mel, a little bit off to the side; me, alongside my father, feeling proud as hell and on top of my game.

When the anthem wrapped and the fans started to whip them-selves into the last of their pregame frenzy, my father turned to me and shook my hand and said, "Go get 'em, Ronnie."

As fine, sweet moments go, this one was right up there, the way it brought me together with the man who'd taken me to my first big league ball game, *at this very stadium*. It was more than I could have ever hoped for, more than I could have ever imagined. If a screenwriter pitched this scene to a Hollywood producer as a turning point moment in a Kevin Costner–ish movie about fathers and sons and baseball, he (or she!) would be dismissed as a hack.

And yet . . . and yet . . . , there it was.

Turned out, I had a helluva game after this close encounter with my father. I threw seven shutout innings, to help put the Mets in position to win the game 6–2 and to even the series at two games apiece, and forever after it felt to me like the moment had been heaven-sent by the baseball gods.

Cal's story started *way* before he put on a big league uniform. He'd grown up in the Orioles organization, where his father, Cal Ripken Sr., had been a longtime coach. When Baltimore drafted him with the twenty-fourth pick of the 1978 draft, both Cals were elated. Cal Jr. finally made it to the Opening Day roster in 1982. His father was in the third base coaching box. And what did Cal Jr. do? First time up, one out, Ken Singleton on second, he smacked his first major league home run, and collected what has got to be one of the finest, sweetest *attaboys* in the history of the game as he rounded third.

Another blessing from the baseball gods, I'm betting.

10

The Only Living Boy in New York

One of the great offshoots to a Manhattan-centric baseball career is the way it introduces you to an aspect of
the city and its denizens you might not normally get to
experience—and, relatedly, the way the city itself seems to look
back at you in kind.

You'll see I've pinched a lyric from an old Simon & Garfunkel
song to stand as the title to this chapter, because during my formative years in the city I really did feel like a kid in a candy
store. There were times in there when I couldn't believe my good
fortune, to be a professional baseball player living in the greatest
city in the world, and it felt to me like I was walking the streets
in a kind of movie montage, with Artie Garfunkel singing the
soundtrack:

Hey, I've got nothing to do today but smile.

Indeed, the points of connection that found me away from Shea Stadium were very often as formative as the relationships that were built on the game itself . . .

For example, I was fortunate at the front end of my time in a uniform to throw in with **Anthony J. Ferrara**, one of the great characters of the game. Tony had been a successful model and a struggling actor before he somehow wangled a gig as the Mets' batting practice pitcher. He also threw BP for the Yankees, so he took the mound pretty much every day during baseball season.

Tony was a character of the first rank. He had a closetful of Oleg Cassini suits—he used to model them back in the 1960s and '70s, and the suits still fit him perfectly. In a lot of ways, he was my spirit guide to city life when I first joined the team. He knew all the best spots for sushi, steaks, drinks, after-hours merrymaking, and he seemed to know everybody in town. In fact, I don't think I ever met a bouncer or maître d' in Tony's presence who didn't greet him by name—even when they were disinclined to wave him (us!) past their velvet rope.

The thing about Tony was he wasn't much of a batting practice pitcher. How he got these two premier gigs was never made clear. He used to pitch for the University of Miami, had always dreamed of making it to the bigs, and I guess this was as far as he got. It wasn't everything, but it was something, were it not for the fact that everyone on our team used to grouse that he was probably one of the worst batting practice pitchers of all time. I can't say for sure how he was regarded up in the Bronx, but some of my Mets teammates wanted to run him out of town.

See, when you're throwing BP, the key is to keep the ball true and straight. Tony's ball moved all over the place. And then it moved some more. There was some sink to it, and his control wasn't the best. I remember how pissed Keith Hernandez would be after a session with Tony, because Tony would make him work for his cuts. And yet somehow Tony managed to hold on to these two jobs for over ten years. For dear life, he held on to them. In fact, Tony was so pleased with his unique status as the batting practice pitcher for New York's two professional baseball teams, he used to keep a running count of the total number of pitches he threw in his sessions. The reasons for this were also never made clear, and yet each day he'd update the number in this little notebook he used to carry. No one was more impressed with the total than Tony himself. Surely, he had one of the great rubber arms in the game, because each round of BP ran to well over two hundred pitches, and when you're throwing on back-to-back days, all season long without let up, that can lead to some serious wear and tear.

We called Tony "The Coach," because that's what he aspired to be, but in reality he wasn't cut out to coach players at the major league level. Later on, Tony found success (and fulfillment) coaching youth baseball, and there the moniker applied, but with us he was more like the guy we loved to razz about his ineffectiveness as a batting practice pitcher. Still, he became a kind of mentor to me—a little like Clarence in that great Frank Capra movie *It's a Wonderful Life,* which I guess cast me as Jimmy Stewart. Tony would show me the ropes in and around town. He used to love to take me down to Little Italy, to this neighborhood bakery he knew, where he taught me about the cookies I was supposed to eat with my double espresso. (Little known fact: every time someone pours a shot of Sambuca into a cup of espresso an angel gets its wings!) He taught me the difference between Sicilian cuisine and Northern Italian cuisine, and showed me where to find the best slice of pizza in the city.

It was Tony who introduced me to Jerry Casale's place, Pino's, where I ended up taking most of my meals during my first couple years in the bigs.

Tony had the city wired, and knew how to work every angle. His angling didn't always achieve the desired result, but he worked those angles just the same. He was constantly running around our clubhouse with a ball or a bat or some other piece of memorabilia he needed signed for this or that charity auction, although we always suspected that this or that charity was Tony himself. After you live in New York for a while, you collect an assortment of friends and gadabouts who don't seem to have a discernible source of income. Tony was that kind of guy—he could have written a book on how to live in Manhattan on $5 a day . . . and then sell you a copy for $10.

Once, he came to our house for Christmas dinner, about a year or two after my oldest son, Tyler, was born. Tony wasn't the type to show up for Christmas dinner empty-handed, and sure enough he'd brought something along for Tyler: a giveaway day helmet from a Yankee Stadium promotion. The fact that the helmet was a freebie didn't bother me or surprise me—that was Tony's way—but it was an adult helmet.

(Hey, it's the thought that counts, and Tony had clearly put some thought into this one—not a lot, but some.)

He used to drive a tiny Honda Accord, which for reasons having nothing to do with his association with the Mets was painted orange. We called the car the Orange Crush, for reasons having less to do with the soda brand than with the surprising lack of leg room it offered a professional athlete. For years, Tony drove me to the stadium—only, finding the car on game day could be an adventure, especially following a particularly rough night on the town, when the car could have been left anywhere. Back in the prehistoric 1980s, there was no way to stay in constant touch with another person. Without cell phones, we couldn't snap a pic to remind our drunk-ass selves where we might have parked the car the night before. We couldn't text each other, as we split up and circled the neighborhood, looking for clues. I could only sit by the phone in my apartment and wait for Tony's call.

And when the call from Tony finally came in, it followed the usual patterns . . .

Me: "What time we headed out?"

Coach: "Three o'clock."

Me: "Where's the Crush?"

Coach: "I'll have to get back to you."

You'd think an orange vehicle would stand out as we walked up and down the block looking for the car, but the Crush was so small you couldn't just peer around the corner and survey the street because it was always tucked into the tiniest spot, between a couple moving vans or delivery trucks.

That apartment, by the way, factored into my emerging sense of quintessential New York–iness as well. During my second year in the bigs, I lived with fellow pitcher **Tim Leary**, who was one of my closest friends on the team until he was traded to the Brewers before the start of the 1985 season. We lived in a two-bedroom unit on the corner of 33rd Street and Third Avenue, and we used to love telling people our address for the way it gave us a chance to slip into our mock New York City accents and say we were at "Toity-toid and Toid."

Tony knew the manager, Rudy Riska, at the Downtown Athletic Club, a private social club and gym in the financial district that I'd only heard of because they awarded the Heisman Trophy every year—one of those New York institutions I never would have discovered on my own were it not for Tony. Rudy would let us work out there. We had the run of the place—one of the great perks of knowing Tony, although I suppose it didn't hurt that I pitched for the Mets. Tony was in tremendous shape. At the time, I assumed we were about the same age, but it turned out he had more than twenty years on me. We'd lift weights, use the sauna, play hoops. For a while, we were in a regular game with **Kevin Dillon** and **Matt Dillon**, around the time Matt's acting career was starting to pop with *The Outsiders* and *The Flamingo Kid*. (Kevin's career wouldn't really take off until *Entourage* in 2004, although he worked pretty steadily in smaller roles throughout my time with the Mets.) They weren't the tallest guys on the court, but the Dillon brothers had game. They were tenacious. We ran full-court, and we ran hard. There was a standing game at noon for all the Wall Street guys, and the caliber of ball was competitive, but they were always out the door by 12:58. If you wanted to keep playing, there was another full-court game that started up around three o'clock. Tony didn't usually stay for the later game, but we mixed it up pretty good with the "Masters of the Universe" and the Dillon brothers.

Tony's New York wasn't exactly "A-list" New York, but at least he was on the list. If going to the Oak Bar at the Plaza was the absolute coolest, classiest thing you could do in New York after-hours, Tony would find the fourth or fifth absolute coolest, classiest thing for us to do instead.

When I was doing the town with Tony, we never quite made it to the big table at Elaine's, the famed bar and nightclub on the Upper East Side run by the legendary restaurateur **Elaine Kaufman** and frequented by heavy hitters like Woody Allen, Gay Talese, Norman Mailer, and Jackie O. Even on my own, or in the company of my fellow Mets, I rarely had the gravitas to be seated front and center, but Elaine always greeted me warmly, generously. She wasn't so kind or welcoming to everybody, so I counted it a blessing when she would get up from her seat and cross the restaurant to give me a hug. Elaine was a big woman, as her favored patrons will surely recall, and I don't offer up that observation to be impolite but to highlight how grateful I always was when she made the effort to stand and greet me—no easy thing for her, I'm afraid.

In those days, a hug from Elaine was a sign that you had arrived . . . although as we passed that big table in front with all those luminaries, and then all those lesser and lesser tables as you moved toward the back, with those lesser and lesser luminaries, I was reminded of how far I still had to go. Once, she sat me down at the big table next to the actor **Chris Noth**, well before he had his first real star turns in *Law & Order* and *Sex and the City*. This was back when he was still in a soap opera and had just joined the cast of *Hill Street Blues*. Still, I thought it was a sign of where I was in this particular pecking order of New York City nightlife celebrity. Yes, I was at the big table at Elaine's, but so was Chris Noth, so it could only mean that it was a slow night on the town. A couple nights later, when the restaurant was a little busier, Elaine escorted me right past the big table, and then right past the next table, until she found a seat for me at a third-tier table . . . once again, right next to Chris Noth, so years later I could flash back on that night and content myself with the thought that even though my star had apparently fallen it had done so in lockstep with a genuine heartthrob.

Mondays in the city would typically find us at "oldies" night at Heartbreak, a disco on Varick Street. The night would usually start with a late dinner at Marylou's, an Italian joint on West Ninth Street that was a popular hangout for artists, athletes, and celebrities. We used to go there to see all the models who'd hang around and pretend to eat Marylou's famous chicken.

Another favorite hang was the China Club, where **Chazz Palminteri** used to work as a bouncer. We got to know each other, over time, and on some nights we'd find ourselves on the street outside the club just shooting the shit. Someone would ask Chazz what he had going on away from the club, and he'd say, "Oh, I'm workin' on somethin'. I'm workin' on a story."

Chazz would tell everyone in those days that he wasn't planning on being a bouncer forever, said he was going make it as a writer. We would look at him and laugh and say, "Yeah, right." To us, Chazz was just another colorful character on the New York scene, but then, a couple years later, his one-man show *A Bronx Tale* opened off-Broadway and was later adapted into a movie with Robert DeNiro—so, yeah, I guess he was working on something.

One of the trademark features of the China Club was this giant aquarium they had over the bar. Every night, a couple drinks in, I'd get to thinking that at some point, sooner or later, somebody would have one too many or say the wrong thing to the wrong person at just the wrong time and a glass or a bottle would get tossed straight through those aquarium walls.

Never happened, but there was always the chance that it could, which kept things interesting.

There was a pecking order at the China Club, too. The place was dominated by a giant bar, with two mezzanine seating areas and a huge dance floor. You'd be seated or situated depending on who you were or where you were in your career. If you were somebody, you sat on the right part of the mezzanine. If you were not quite somebody, and yet a notch or two up from being a nobody, you sat on the left side of the mezzanine. If you were merely a wannabe and in reality nobody at all, you were relegated to the dance floor. Most nights, we'd take our place on the right, but we would be seated on the left from time to time when our visit might have overlapped with a group of someones a little more worthy of this particular sliver of limelight.

(Oh, and speaking of Limelight . . . that was another New York hot spot during my early years with the Mets—a converted church in Chelsea that was turned into a nightclub that on some nights was as wild as wild could be.)

Tony's Orange Crush was my standard ride to Shea Stadium in those days, but he almost never drove me home. He'd typically leave after the third inning or so, and we'd catch up with him after the game. There were just a few of us on the team living in Manhattan during my first couple years with the Mets, so we'd roll together back to the city. After most games, that meant hopping into the delivery van Rusty Staub would repurpose from his Upper East Side restaurant. We used to call it the Emerson Fittipaldi Brazilian Rib Machine. As I wrote earlier, Rusty was good to his word when he promised Frank Cashen that he'd look after me, and ferry me back to the city after our home games—only he never said anything about ferrying me around in style. Rusty's ride was a beaten-down, graffiti-strewn commercial van that looked like something Shaggy would drive to a haunted house on *Scooby-Doo*. It was used all day by Rusty's crew to haul slabs of beef and pork, and someone would drop it off at Shea so he could drive himself home after the game. (There was no refrigeration unit in the van, as I recall, so on hot summer days it could get pretty rank in there!) There was a bucket seat for a passenger up front, but the rear of the van had been stripped bare to accommodate Rusty's daily deliveries, so we sat on the metal runners in the cargo area, or on milk crates. Rusty would drive, and Keith Hernandez would ride shotgun, and I'd pile into the back of the van with Tim Leary, Danny Heep, and Ed Lynch—our Manhattan contingent.

Rusty was famous among our group for being incredibly cheap—and deathly afraid of heights. What this meant as far as our reverse commute was concerned was that we'd never take the Triborough Bridge or the Midtown Tunnel back into the city because he didn't want to pay the tolls, so we'd head for the 59th Street Bridge. Trouble was, on some nights the traffic would be rerouted in such a way that we'd have to take the outside lane. That always freaked Rusty out, to be driving at the very edge of the bridge, so perilously close to the water. He couldn't take it, so whenever that happened he'd stop the car, stop traffic, and hop out of the driver's seat. He wouldn't even say anything. He'd just throw the car into park, get out, and walk around to the passenger seat, and it was up to one of us to take the wheel. Keith would never drive, so it fell to me or Danny or Eddie.

Most nights, we'd head directly to Rusty's restaurant on 73rd and Third. We'd get a bite to eat and throw back a couple beers before heading home, and after a while word got around that Rusty and a few of his teammates were in the habit of eating and drinking there after games. Very quickly, Rusty's place became one of the go-to bars in the city, just on the back of our postgame routine. The restaurant was always busy, during lunch and dinner hours, but the fact that you could swing by late at night and maybe join a few of your Metsies for a drink kicked things up a notch—changed the whole vibe, really.

And so began my foray into the life of the city. Very quickly, I started thinking of myself as a New Yorker—no small leap, considering my New England roots, especially when it came to the local sports scene.

Following my first full season with the Mets, I treated myself to season tickets to the Knicks and Rangers. I couldn't really afford it, but I wanted to support my fellow New York athletes and sit with the fans when it wasn't my ass on the line, so Madison Square Garden was like my second home that winter. The Knicks weren't very good in those days, but they had the great Bernard King, before he blew out his knee and had to miss a couple seasons. The Rangers weren't very good, either, although they seemed to always make the playoffs.

One of the things I loved about this season ticket setup was that the Garden was right across town from my apartment. I could just head directly west from our front door and be in my seat twenty minutes later—to me, just then, this was the coolest thing in the world, to be able to walk to a game and not worry about traffic or parking. It's like I'd died and gone to heaven, if I could forget for a moment that I was now root, root, rooting for my adopted hometown teams.

One of the other things I loved was the way New York fans seemed to embrace the same type of gritty, hard-nosed player. For these Knicks, that player was Ernie Grunfeld—a kid from Queens who got by on determination. He didn't get a whole lot of minutes, but whenever the Knicks were down big at the end of the game, the crowd started chanting Ernie's name. He'd come in, make a big play, and the place would just go nuts.

Nick Fotiu filled the same kind of role for the Rangers—a kid from Staten Island, the Rangers' first homegrown player, who was usually called on to act as the team's enforcer. Whenever he dropped his gloves and started mixing it up with an opposing player, Ranger fans would lose their shit.

These games were such an education for me, because they helped me to appreciate the mind-set of the New York sports fan. Yeah, the fans expected to you to win, but even more than that they expected you to bust your butt. To dive for a loose ball. To take a punch and give two in return. And as the character of our 1986 championship team was taking shape, I remember wondering how our scrappy, feisty, gritty teammates would be received by the Garden crowd. We had our share of fighters on that team, so I'm pretty sure we would have gotten a hero's welcome.

Those season tickets were a little above my pay grade, just then, but looking back I believe they were a great investment in my card-carrying New Yorker status. I was making the major league minimum salary—$30,000—and my rent back then was $700, so I supplemented my income by filling my off-season weekends with personal appearances. Some of these came through the Mets front office, and some came through guys like Tony Ferrara. After a while, they found me on their own. Bar mitzvahs, Little League banquets . . . whatever the cultural equivalent was for the rubber chicken circuit as it applied to first-year ballplayers, that's what I was on. The going rate in those days was $500, so on a good weekend I could cover my rent and make a dent in those season ticket prices—a win-win, all around.

Once, I shared a limo to the Catskill mountain region north of the city with New York Giants quarterback **Phil Simms**. Phil was a little more established in his career than I was in mine, and yet I found it reassuring to know that I wasn't the only local athlete looking to supplement his income in this way. We were headed to one of the classic Borsch Belt hotels for one of the most over-the-top bar mitzvah celebrations I'd ever seen—because, by this time, I was something of an authority on over-the-top bar mitzvah celebrations. The only thing we knew headed up to the hotel was that the bar mitzvah boy we'd been hired to help celebrate was a major Mets fan and Giants fan, and that he loved the zoo. Clearly, Phil and I had the Mets and Giants part covered, but it was unclear to both of us how the zoo piece would fit into the picture. Well, when we arrived at the hotel, we found out soon enough. In fact, our noses gave the scene away before we could see it for ourselves. There in the grand ballroom of this grand hotel was a menagerie of animals: elephants, giraffes, monkeys. It was the most incongruous thing, to see (and smell!) these beasts in the middle of all this splendor and excess. It was surreal—like a scene from a Fellini movie.

Phil and I flashed each other these *what the hell are we into?* looks.

I said, "You ever see anything like this before?"

He laughed and said, "Rookie." Like he was waving me off. Like such as this was the most natural thing in the world . . . which, in the rarefied air we were now breathing as fledgling New York sports heroes, I suppose it was.

Perhaps the *most* rarefied air I got a chance to breathe as a young professional athlete was in the company of the legendary *Lauren Bacall*—a baseball fan, it turned out. The meeting stemmed from a friendship Keith Hernandez had struck with *Bobby Zarem*, the New York press agent who was widely credited with coming up with the city's famous "I Love New York" campaign.

Bobby was in the habit early on in my career of arranging lunches and dinners with some of New York's movers and shakers—and Keith, who was in the habit of enjoying a fine meal and the company of interesting and influential people away from the game, would often participate. Keith would ask me to join him from time to time, but this wasn't really my thing. I tended to hang back when I was out of my element, and the thought of having to make conversation with these variously successful individuals was a little intimidating . . . that is, until the prospect of dining with Lauren Bacall was on the table.

I'd been a big fan of old movies for as long as I could remember, and of course I knew the special place Bogie and Bacall occupied in the history of American cinema. But I'd never had the chance to meet a Hollywood legend, so of course I jumped at it.

Oh. My. Goodness. Lauren Bacall was such a delightful, captivating presence. A singular beauty, a brassy spirit. The room seemed to tilt on her axis. The first time she spoke, in that deep, gravelly voice, I just about melted. I mumbled something stupid— like, "It's such an honor to meet you, Ms. Bacall."

She responded with something charming and self-effacing—like, "My friends call me Betty."

And I was left to wonder for the next couple beats if this was my invitation to do the same.

Betty knew the game, wanted nothing more than to talk about the Mets' chances and some of the old ballplayers she used to know, but I wanted to pepper her with questions about Bogie and Hollywood.

And so one of the great nights of my early career unfolded in this back-and-forth way—a night that had almost nothing to do with baseball and at the same time almost everything to do with baseball.

We were joined at dinner by my first wife, Toni, and by Keith's girlfriend, Sherri, and there's a picture from that evening that remains one of my most treasured mementos. In fact, I've probably kept just four or five pictures from my playing days, and this is one of them, and what's remarkable about this photo is the sheer star power on display. Think of it: Keith was a good-looking guy, maybe thirty years old, in peak physical condition, looking as good as he would ever look. I was maybe twenty-five, looking as good as I would ever look. Toni and Sherri were both models at the top of their game, looking as good as *they* would ever look. And yet the only person you can really *see* in that picture is Betty Bacall.

It's the strangest, most wonderful thing, the way your eyes are drawn to her. It was that way in the restaurant, the night we met, and it's that way all these years later, when I take out the picture and remember what it was like to begin to move about New York City like I belonged no place else.

Cool-Down

The State of the Game

The more things change, the more they stay the same.

That's a tired old saw that doesn't seem to have a whole lot of teeth in baseball these days, and as I reach back for these stories from my time in the game I can't help but think where the game itself is headed.

I'm a purist at heart. I've never warmed to the idea of the designated hitter, or to interleague play, or even to the instant replay review system implemented in 2014 that granted managers the right to challenge a ruling on the field. Each of these tweaks and modifications seemed to me to take a little bit of the shine off our national pastime, to subtract the human element in favor of a more predictable outcome or a possible bump in attendance, but none of them threatened the very fabric of the sport.

Ah, but that's no longer the case . . .

The increasing reliance on analytics and sabermetrics is fundamentally changing the way the game is played on the field. The nine-figure contracts we dole out to our top-tier players and the mere eight-figure contracts awarded to our second-tier veterans have altered the landscape to where management must coddle the arms of young pitchers, nurture the health of position players, and micromanage their rosters and strategies like never before. Ballplayers are now perceived as bottom-line assets to be preserved and protected, instead of as weapons to be consistently deployed. Today's game—Baseball 2.0—doesn't even *look* like the game I used to play, at times. I've talked about this in the booth at length, but it feels appropriate to close this collection of anecdotes about the players and personalities who've crossed my path with a look at some of the ways the game has evolved . . . and at the ways today's players and personalities are made to adapt to what has essentially been a front-office evolution.

Consider the way the stolen base has fallen out of favor in recent years—in part because of the desire to prolong the careers of star players who might run themselves down over time (you know, with all that sliding), but mostly because the numbers now tell us that the stolen base is only effective if you're able to succeed 80 percent of the time. This may, in fact, be so, but it doesn't account for the fact that even the game's greatest base stealers had to struggle early on before figuring out how to run on major league pitchers. It's like anything else—you learn your craft by learning from your mistakes. You have to get thrown out a time or two, take some chances, before you find your way, but there doesn't seem to be any room in today's game for a manager to allow his fleet-footed base runners to take their lumps.

Consider the way teams try to manage their pitchers by babying their arms and squeezing their pitch counts. Sure, I understand that when you sign a pitcher to a big contract you want to protect your investment—but what are you protecting him for, exactly? His Age 32 season? There was a stretch of games early in the 2018 season that helped to put this approach into perspective. ***Jacob deGrom***, the Mets' All-Star pitcher, in the first weeks of an historic Cy Young–winning season, left a scoreless game against the Braves in the fourth inning with a hyperextended elbow. (He'd thrown just 46 pitches, by the way.) The Mets, not wanting to take any chances with such an important arm, put deGrom on the disabled list as a precaution, allowing him to miss his next start. When he returned to the rotation ten days later in Philadelphia, he struggled to get through the first inning, throwing 45 pitches while still managing to keep the Phillies off the scoreboard. (Such a competitor!) As a further precaution, the Mets took him out of the game. What that meant was that the team was essentially shelving their ace for three consecutive starts—roughly 10 percent of his projected workload for the season. And for what? Yes, deGrom came back from these precautions and was absolutely untouchable, pitching to a 1.23 ERA over his next seven starts, even though the anemic Mets offense could only help him to win two of those ball games, but as I watched this drama unfold I couldn't shake thinking that something was off in the way the team was using one of the game's best pitchers.

Let's not forget, the decision on how and when, and at what capacity to use a player, is never made in a vacuum. It's made by a many-headed team that includes the organization, the player, the player's agent, and the Player's Association, with some second-guessing thrown in by the fans and beat writers. To my mind, when you're blessed with a twenty-nine-year-old ace like deGrom, the thing to do is pitch him. A lot. I don't care what the analytics say. History tells us that you have to play your guys ragged until age catches up to them. After that, whatever you get out of them is a bonus. Before that, whatever you get out of him is what you're paying for—and what the Mets were paying for in deGrom was a season of sustained brilliance. Would those three squandered starts have changed the team's fortunes for the season? Hardly, but that's not the point. It's kind of like digging deep to invest in a classic car, and then leaving it to gather dust in the garage. Take the thing out for a spin and see what it can do.

Consider, too, the way managers now routinely deploy the defensive shift throughout the game, on a situational basis. When I was a kid, you only saw the shift against guys like Boog Powell or Willie McCovey—and even then, you wouldn't see it *every* time those guys stepped to the plate. It was an outlier-type move, dismissed by a lot of traditional baseball minds back then as little more than a stunt. When I was a player, you'd put on the shift only on rare occasions—against certain players, in certain situations. Here again this was the exception, not the rule.

Nowadays, though, you might see the shift a couple times each half-inning, which can sometimes mean more often than not, and what's interesting to me is that nobody really talks about the impact this type of maneuvering can have on a pitcher's effectiveness, and his ability to execute to his strengths. Let's forget for a moment how a guy who's spent his entire career at third might have a difficult time adjusting to a ground ball hit to the right side of the infield. I understand that if the numbers say this is where the guy hits the ball the majority of time, that's where you have to put your gloves. But I don't understand how organizations consistently take the ball out of their best pitchers' hands and force them to adhere to this newfangled playbook—because, let's face it, in order to be successful *against* the shift, you're asking your pitchers to make pitches that allow the ball to be hit *into* the shift, a construct that might be antithetical to the skill set that earned those pitchers a spot on a major league roster in the first place.

Here, let me break it down:

I was a guy who liked to sink the ball away from a left-handed hitter, forcing him to hit the ball on the ground. If you look at the numbers over my career, in these righty-lefty matchups, that meant *way* more ground balls than fly balls. It didn't mean *no* fly balls, but the dominant outcome, if the batter put the ball in play, was on the ground, and most of *those* balls were grounded weakly to our shortstop or third baseman. In today's game, if we're playing the shift against a dangerous left-hander, you've taken away my most important pitch. A sinking fastball away is the easiest ball for a left-handed hitter to hit to the left side of the infield—so just like that, my strength becomes a weakness, because four of my infield gloves will have been aligned on the right side of the infield.

The problem is there are very few pitchers in today's game who have the gravitas or the résumé to push back against such as this. Sure, if you're Justin Verlander your manager and your pitching coach will listen to you if you point out that you've had success against this or that left-handed hitter who mostly hits the ball to short. But if you're a young pitcher, there's no arguing with organizational strategy. You can either go with the flow or step off the mound.

Relatedly, as the game leans more and more toward limited pitch counts for young starters, we're seeing more and more five- or six-inning pitchers. It becomes a self-fulfilling prophecy, because once you start shutting down these pitchers after the second time through the order, you never condition their arms to go any deeper in a game.

What this means, over time, is that the game is starting to produce a generation of pitchers who are able to pitch to the analytics, and that's it. When they pitch to the analytics and get a positive result, that means a win. It means the process has been considered and dealt with. It means they get to keep their jobs as major league pitchers, and the generous paychecks that attach to those jobs. It means they've been given a blueprint for success, and if they stick to the plan they'll be rewarded for it, even if the opposing team manages to scratch out a couple hits, or bunt against the shift, or offer up some kind of counterpunch strategy of their own. As long as they pitch to the process, they've covered their asses.

But it's not really about covering your ass, is it?

I'm thinking back to a left-handed hitter like **Will Clark**, who for comparison purposes will stand in here as the Bryce Harper of my day. Remember Will's picture-perfect, loping swing? It was a thing of beauty, but you could pitch to him. In my case, that meant my sinker down and away. If I was facing him with a shift behind me, however, I'd have to throw him a cutter or a breaking ball that he could pull. He'd be more likely to be out in front of that pitch, particularly if he knew I couldn't throw my sinker, so my only hope would be to induce him to hit the ball into the teeth of my defense. That would give me the best chance.

Of course, analytics of this type are nothing new. Corner infielders have always guarded the lines late in the game; outfielders have always played deep against power hitters, and shallow against spray hitters, and shaded left or right against the pull; infielders would hang back at double-play depth or draw in for a potential play at the plate, depending on the situation. Even as kids scrambling to get a pickup game together, we knew when we were shortsided and didn't have enough players to field two full teams to set it up so that a ball hit to right field by a right-handed hitter would be an automatic out. A ball hit to left field by a left-handed hitter, same thing. And we'd position our players accordingly. But by making the opposite field out of bounds, we were somehow able to *preserve* the integrity of the game, because there was no room in our ground rules for a soft liner the other way to fall for a cheap hit. You had to beat the other team, not outsmart them. That's no longer the case at the big league level, where it sometimes seems our overreliance on analytics has *perverted* the integrity of the game, to where it's now possible to beat the other team by going against time-honored baseball culture. It used to be that you weren't supposed to bunt against the shift, or late in the game if you were down by more than three runs, but all of that is out the window in today's game.

That cheap hit, for those players smart enough to grab at it, has become a game-changer.

Case in point: as I write this, the Mets are coming off a game where their veteran shortstop-turned-second-baseman **Asdrubal Cabrera** came to the plate with the score tied, late, runner on second, nobody out. The opposing team put on a full infield shift, leaving one defender on the left side of the infield at the traditional shortstop position, shaded toward second. The way baseball has always been played, Asdrubal would have given himself up in that spot and attempted to lay down a sacrifice bunt, which would have likely advanced the runner to third. The way the game is now played, however, Asdrubal was able to smartly push the ball to the left side for an infield hit, leaving the Mets with runners on first *and* third, still with nobody out. The next batter, Wilmer Flores, drove the ball to right field for a sacrifice fly, bringing the runner home and leaving me to scratch my head in the booth and wonder at what the game has become.

That same week, the Mets were up 1–0 against the Marlins. Top of the sixth, two outs. The Marlins' Starlin Castro singled to center off Mets reliever Paul Sewald, who then walked Brian Anderson, putting runners on first and second. The Mets brought on their left-handed specialist Jerry Blevens to face the Marlins' slugging first baseman Justin Bour, a left-handed hitter, so the Mets of course put on the shift. (It's become a knee-jerk reaction!) With only one defender on the left side of the infield, in the shortstop position, Castro was able to *walk* to third for one of the most maddening stolen bases I'd ever seen at the major league level. I couldn't understand it. For the Mets to be so confident in their one-run lead, and in their numbers, to practically invite the runner on second to cross over to third, where he would now be in a position to score on a passed ball . . . it made no sense to me, from a by-the-book baseball perspective.

And yet, here we were. Here we *are*.

Just to finish out the inning, Bour walked to load the bases, and Blevens was pulled from the game after throwing just six pitches. A. J. Ramos then came on to strike out pinch hitter Derek Dietrich to end the inning—meaning, I guess, that the Mets had kept the Marlins off the board, so the analytics had somehow won out.

As we went to commercial, I said something to Gary about how the powers that be in today's game were certainly smart, and allowed that their constant maneuvering and manipulating of the usual baseball tactics might often produce the desired outcome, but they were making the game unwatchable.

The game has changed off the field as well. In my day, if you didn't speak to the manager or the general manager all year, you had a good season. Today's player needs an open line of communication with his manager at all times. Sometimes, that open line of communication is intensely scrutinized, with the way we've got our cameras poised to capture every conceivable moment, from every conceivable angle, and with the way fans and sportswriters are so quick to weigh in with note and comment on social media.

Remember that clash of wills between Mets ace **Matt Harvey** and manager **Terry Collins** that played out in the dugout during Game 5 of the 2015 World Series? That would have played out a little differently in my day, when ballplayers had a different sense of self-importance. Here's how it played out in this one: the Mets were down 3–1 in the Series. Harvey was the alpha dog of the staff, coming off of Tommy John surgery. The organization had pinned its hopes on this young man's reconstituted arm, with a season-long cap on his innings, and now the Series rode on his arm as well. He was the face of the franchise, with the swagger to match. And he was fairly dominant on this night at Citi Field, taking a 2–0 lead into the top of the eighth, whereupon he dispatched Paulo Orlando, Alcides Escobar, and Ben Zobrist on just nine pitches.

This was where the clash of wills came in. (And those cameras!) As the fans stood and cheered and Harvey stepped back into the dugout, Mets pitching coach Dan Warthen crossed to shake his hand, congratulate him on his fine outing, and tell him he was done for the night. Harvey bristled, as alpha dogs with swagger are wont to do, and the television crews picked up on the exchange. Viewers at home could see Harvey mouth the words "No way!" The CitiField fans on the third base side of the stadium could see their star pitcher become heated, animated as hell, and march over to his manager.

It didn't take a veteran analyst or color commentator or lip reader to see what was going on. Any seasoned fan could tell that Harvey was pleading his case, pushing every button he could to get his manager to leave him in the game.

What you had here was a kind of perfect storm of moment and emotion. You had a young, cocky pitcher who'd been through a lot, who'd battled back from an incredible injury and was pushing himself to a place innings-wise and timetable-wise that no other pitcher ever had reached following Tommy John surgery. You had a baseball man who was old enough to remember a time when a manager looked into his players' eyes and read the fire inside, instead of looking at spreadsheets that spoke to him only of trends and tendencies and percentages. And you had an era of intense media scrutiny—broadcast and social—that placed this back-and-forth in a harsh spotlight.

"I want this game," Harvey said. "I want it bad."

So Collins set aside the analytics, ignored Harvey's pitch count (101), and ran his ace back to the mound for the ninth—later telling reporters that he let his heart get in the way of his gut.

As Mets fans will never forget, the Royals' Lorenzo Cain worked out a walk to lead off the ninth. Cain then stole second, and came home on a double off the bat of Eric Hosmer, and that was it for Harvey. Jeurys Familia came on to close things out, but he couldn't quite get the job done, allowing Hosmer to cross to third on an infield grounder and then to score on what might have been the second out of a 5–3–2 double play.

Harvey's fine outing was effectively erased—and the Mets ended up losing the game, and the Series, when the Royals erupted for five runs in the top of the 12th inning.

Collins and Harvey both came under fire for their roles in this drama—roles that were magnified because they were acted out on such a public stage. Collins was ripped by the fans and by the media for not following the script, and allowing his hotheaded pitcher to call the shots. Harvey was ripped for being that hotheaded pitcher, a little too full of himself to accept the decisions of his coaches and manager. And yet for generations, ballplayers and managers without the benefit of all those spreadsheets might have gone through these same motions in essentially the same way, without any blowback or fallout. I can't tell you how many times a manager wanted to pull me from the game, and I was able to look him in the eye and say, "Skip, I got this one." There was no disrespect, only confidence. I saw it from my teammates all the time—from opposing pitchers, too. It was the way of the game. And the manager would give you that rope, if he thought you could use it to climb your way out of whatever jam you were in; or, he wouldn't, if he thought you'd hang yourself with it.

It wasn't that Terry Collins let his heart get in the way of his gut. It was that his heart *and* his gut got into his head. His pitcher got into his head. And the baseball world was watching, ready to second-guess him, no matter which way he turned.

Look, I'm not a big fan of playing to the script managers tend to write out in their heads before each game, trying to anticipate every conceivable situation—and, in some cases, even some *inconceivable* situations.

Here's how that script might have gone:

Harvey would have been pulled after the eighth for Familia, because the book said that would give the Mets the best chance to win.

Collins would have stepped to his ace and shaken his hand and said, "Great game, Matt."

Harvey might have pushed back a little, competitor that he was, and said, "I've got to have this game."

Collins might have said, "I'd love you to have this game, but not tonight."

And that would have been that. Except it wasn't.

Now, Bill Walsh, the great head coach of the San Francisco 49ers, was famous for scripting the first twenty, twenty-five plays of every game, and there's no arguing with his team's success. The problem with scripting a baseball game, though, is that there are too many variables in play. There's no room in the ebb and flow of the game to plan out which relievers will face which hitters in which situations. In football, if you go three and out on one possession, you're gifted a new set of downs on the next possession—a clean slate. In baseball, there are no clean slates. What would have happened if Collins followed the script and Familia came on to face those three tough hitters to start the ninth and he ended up walking the first two? That kind of gets you off script, right? And yet today's managers, more and more, are sticking to the plan. Why? Because they're no different from the young pitchers who pitch to the analytics to cover their asses; they want to keep their jobs. Because today's managers are more like middle managers. Their role is to act as a kind of field director for the general manager and his staff, to execute an organization's overall game plan, and to do so by whatever book that organization has chosen to follow. And, as such, they're easily replaced.

Of course, I'm generalizing here. Of course, there are exceptions to this line of thinking. There are outstanding managers like Mike Scioscia, Terry Francona, Joe Maddon, Bruce Bochy, and on and on who have a long history on the bench and the rope they need to call their own games, but if you look at the trend across the game in managerial hires you'll see big league skippers getting younger and younger, with less and less coaching experience under their belts and more and more of an affinity for numbers and percentages. They're as comfortable talking statistics with baseball wonks as they are teaching their players the benefits of playing the percentages. At some point, I'm afraid, all thirty teams will have the same manager. They'll be young—mid-forties, able to communicate with their also-young players. They'll have had a modest playing career, but an extensive résumé in analytics, and years of service as a kind of conduit between the general manager's office and the clubhouse. The way things are going, I can even envision a scenario where we'll see a manager with absolutely no playing experience—something that would have never seemed possible back in my day, and now seems not only likely but an inevitable extension of where the game is headed.

(Hey, in this era of driverless cars, Google might even come up with a model for a manager-less team!)

This very public Matt Harvey–Terry Collins exchange stands at a kind of midpoint for how these conversations have gone in the past, between players and management, and how they might go in the future. It puts me in mind of the one time I can remember from my own career when I got a little heated when a manager wanted to take me out of the game. It happened during the 1990 season, after the Mets fired Davey Johnson when the team got off to a 20–22 start. The feeling in the organization was that Davey had allowed the mood of our clubhouse to become a little too fast and loose for our own good, so **Bud Harrelson** was brought on to kind of keep his thumb on the free spirits among us and set things right. And it turned out to be the right move on the part of management, because we went 71–49 the rest of the way—good for a second-place finish in the NL East.

Early on in Buddy's tenure, I got myself into a rough spot during a game at Wrigley. The bases were loaded and Ryne Sandberg was due up. Buddy came out to the mound to take my temperature—which, as you'll see, was pretty damn hot.

Typically, you'd send out the pitching coach when the visit to the mound was to buy time for your bullpen to get ready or to settle a pitcher, but here Mel Stottlemyre had stayed on the bench, so at first I thought I was getting the hook. But Buddy just wanted to talk—he said, "I'm feeling like I got to take you out. You got anything left for me?"

For whatever reason, the comment set me off. The whole scenario set me off. Buddy had brought the entire infield out to the mound with him, and he was up in my face, and it just wasn't the way to play it with a veteran pitcher in the heat of competition. With *this* veteran pitcher in the heat of competition. So I lit into Buddy, for no good reason beyond the fact that I'd chosen to be offended by his approach. I said, "Buddy, what the fuck have you been watching the last ten years? Get the fuck off my mound."

Happily, mercifully, graciously . . . he did. He left me in the ball game, too, and I somehow managed to get out of the inning, and we never spoke of the incident again. Buddy had been a fixture with the Mets for over forty years, not counting brief stops in Philadelphia and Texas at the end of his playing career. I loved the guy, and it killed me that I went after him in this way, and it's killed me over the years that I never said anything to him about it. I should have apologized, but despite my bluster on the mound I was too chickenshit to apologize, and our relationship became a little strained after that.

It's one of the great regrets of my career that I spoke to my manager in this way. That I spoke to my friend in this way. It was my own little Matt Harvey moment, and I offer it here as a reminder that there has always been a kind of tug-and-pull between players and management. What was different here in Game 5 of the 2015 World Series was that it played out in such a public way. What was different, too, was that Bud Harrelson and I had a relationship, a history. I respected who he was as a player, and understood what he meant to the organization and its fans. We were connected to each other by the stitches in the knitting of the Mets franchise, running all the way to those great Dodgers and Giants teams of the 1940s and '50s, to those great Yankees teams up in the Bronx, to the hundreds of legends and characters and miscreants of the game who were connected even in a tenuous way to the game we were playing that day at Wrigley Field.

In some ways, I'm afraid, those connections were not as keenly felt in the thick of tension that sprang up between Matt Harvey and Terry Collins on that November night at Citi Field. Oh, Terry was surely feeling them—he'd been bouncing around professional baseball since 1970, first as a player with the Pirates and Dodgers organizations, and eventually as a manager of the Dodgers' Class A affiliate. But if I had to bet I'd say Matt Harvey wasn't feeling them quite so much. This is not a knock on Harvey so much as it is another one of my sweeping generalizations made from on high, up in the broadcast booth. Today's young players don't seem to be connected to the game the way we were, the way players *always* were . . . until now. And that is a shame. I'd suggest here that it is a *crying* shame, but we've already covered that: there is no crying in baseball. And yet it is a shame nonetheless, for it is in the threads of the game that we take our measure as ballplayers. Pull on one thread and it will lead you to another . . . and to another one after that. Pull on enough of them, and your own game can begin to take shape.

The more things change, the more they stay the same.

Maybe there's a little more truth to that line than I thought at first. We go 'round and 'round in this game, after all. What's in favor one season is out of favor the next. The stolen base waxes and wanes. The long ball is prized, until someone comes along and convinces us that the percentages have leaned in favor of a *small ball* approach. The shift, perhaps, will come and go.

What remains will be the characters of the game . . . the *character* of the game . . . the game itself.

Index

Index